THE WRITING ROAD TO READING

THE
WRITING
ROAD
TO
READING

A Modern Method of Phonics for
Teaching Children to Read

By
Romalda Bishop Spalding
with
Walter T. Spalding

WHITESIDE, INC., AND WILLIAM MORROW & COMPANY
Revised Edition
NEW YORK, 1962

CONTENTS

65367

INTRODUCTION

THE PURPOSE of this book is to present in complete and workable detail the Unified Phonics Method for teaching children correct and accurate speech, writing, spelling, and reading. This is the method which I have developed and used exclusively during the past twenty-five years. Throughout this period of vigorous testing—in all the elementary grades and in the tutoring of hundreds of individuals with language disabilities—I have found it equally applicable to *home* and *school* use, and as practicable for a single pupil as for an entire class. And though the method was designed especially for use in the elementary schools beginning with the first grade, it has proved to be fully successful in high school classrooms and in private instruction from pre-school age through college age, and even older. Indeed, anyone with a deficiency in reading and spelling can benefit from the Unified Phonics Method regardless of age.

At the outset I think it important to state several things which the method is *not:*

It does *not* advocate the old-fashioned phonics commonly taught thirty years ago and now being partially revived in many American schools.

The Unified Phonics Method, with its new approach and its im-

7

proved, accurate, simplified phonics, is *not* merely a useful adjunct to the whole-word, or sight method of teaching.

The Unified Phonics Method has proved its usefulness for children with language deficiencies, but it is *not* primarily a technique for remedial reading—that costly, widespread and frightening proof of the faulty teaching of beginning readers today.

It is *not* merely another alternate and theoretical approach to the reading problem.

The Unified Phonics Method *is* a fully developed, highly successful method for teaching the basic techniques of the language—accurate speaking, spelling, writing and reading—as one integrated subject.

Practical experience has convinced me that any child physically and mentally qualified to enter school at the age of six is fully able, willing and eager to learn to write and read if he is taught by this logical approach to language. The professional concept of "reading readiness" is accordingly immaterial. Ideally, therefore, this teaching method should be instituted in the first grade (or kindergarten), and the beginning reader should not be confused by simultaneous exposure to any other method of teaching.

The core of the method is a technique by which the child learns how to write down the sounds used in spoken English as they are combined into words. Thus, conversely he can pronounce any printed word. Meaning is thoroughly taught hand-in-hand with the writing and by using new words in original sentences. It begins with correct pronunciation of words and the writing of their component sounds in accordance with the rules of English spelling. By this means the saying, writing, reading and meaning of words are well learned and understood. After this initial grounding, a child in his reading recognizes words at a glance—very soon without any resort to their phonetic composition. For reading there is no resort to pictures or any other aids except the use of phonics. After a new word has been read aloud its meaning is discussed and pictures are used if they can help explain the meaning. However, looking at pictures is not reading.

Thus far, I have stressed the ideal situation in which the Unified Phonics Method is used exclusively to teach reading to beginners, and as such I recommend it to all elementary school teachers and school systems. As the world knows, elementary school teachers by and large are overworked and underpaid; but also they are dedicated men and women who devote their lives to the all-important task of equipping youngsters with the basic tools of learning. Their finest reward is their pleasure in seeing the eager minds of children develop keenness and strength. If teachers are bewildered by the theories and countertheories that mark the present controversy over the teaching of reading in our schools, if they feel that methods presently in vogue are less than satisfactory for the majority of their pupils, they should find in the Unified Phonics Method the answer to their problems. In similar situations I recommend it to parents who wish to start their children on the road to reading *before* formal schooling begins. For some children, the age of four is not too young.

We live, however, in a real world, and the ideal situation, I realize, will not materialize overnight. Accordingly, therefore, though I have said that the Unified Phonics Method is not primarily intended for remedial or supplementary use, I can also attest to its success when so used. Parents who are troubled by the realization that their children have fallen below the already too low "normal" accomplishments of American school children in reading and writing have here a method which they can practice successfully at home to overcome the deficiency. It is equally valuable to remedial or group teachers at any point.

The book, then, is recommended—and, yes, dedicated—to both teachers and parents. The ultimate dedication, of course, is to the school children of America themselves, whose right it is that they be given the means to master those basic tools of learning, the three R's. Without the three R's the developing and productive use of the mind, the habit of mental self-discipline and self-education, and, indeed, any real appreciation of our cultural heritage are impossible.

There is still some controversy today as to the first objective of the schools' educational program. There are some educators, for example, who argue that the primary, if not sole, aim is the adjustment of the child to his environment. Others argue as strongly that the first consideration in school is learning and intellectual development. I stand with the latter to the extent that I believe that teaching the three R's and other intellectual techniques and disciplines is the first responsibility of our schools. No other agency is charged with this vital task. The social adjustment of each to his fellow is the important duty of parents, but it should be the secondary aim of the teacher because adjustment is a matter equally shared with the home, the church, and other agencies. The formal education of children should be centered on the development of their highest individual ability to reason and think for themselves and on the inculcation of the desire to learn. Their education should also express a deep regard for high standards of work and for high ideals and moral values. The very life of our free world depends upon our children's intellectual development and intellectual integrity.

The attainment of these goals, given the right methods, is perhaps easier than we think. Children need and naturally desire reasoned discipline, strong guidance, and leadership from their elders. They need and want to be held to high standards of performance. And without these things "social adjustment" may well be somewhat meaningless.

I have reached these general conclusions along with my specific teaching method during some twenty-five years of study and work which included the usual courses required of the teaching profession and many advanced courses in the teaching of reading at Columbia and Harvard Universities. I have had continuous practical teaching experience in the Katherine Branson School, California, the Birch-Wathen School, New York, the Bronxville, N.Y. Public Schools, and Shady Hill School, Cambridge. I have taught every elementary grade. In recent years I have devoted all my time to teaching my method on a college staff for college credits and otherwise to large classes of teachers, and some parents, here in Hawaii and in many mainland schools, and as a consultant in charge of the teaching of this method in a large number of private schools. Over the years I have become indebted to many people.

I am basically, and most gratefully, indebted to the late Dr. Samuel T. Orton, eminent neurologist and brain specialist of New York, for his years of research and discoveries and of teaching in this field. It was my privilege, after having taken profitless courses from a number of leaders in the field of reading, to teach a Bronxville school boy directly under Dr. Orton for almost three years. His theory of the functioning of the brain in speaking, writing and reading and his application of this theory to overcome confusions were not only clear and logical but highly effective in practice. His book, READING, WRITING AND SPEECH PROBLEMS IN CHILDREN (W. W. Norton & Company, Inc., New York, 1937) covers this from the medical viewpoint. My contribution has been to organize and expedite the application of his ideas to classroom teaching techniques through the many years of trial and patient practice. The value of Dr. Orton's pioneering work in the field cannot be overestimated.

Many classroom teachers and school principals have taken the forty-hour course I have given on the Unified Phonics Method. They have conducted long and accurate experiments with it. In twenty-four schools in Hawaii and in many schools across the country it is now being used in the elementary grades. To all of these teachers and to their school superintendents, I am deeply indebted. Their devoted study, accurate teaching, and enthusiasm over the results have been a constant satisfaction.

I am grateful also to Mrs. Samuel T. Orton for her permission to use in this book facsimiles of the phonogram cards which I was given by Dr. Orton.

Further, I wish to acknowledge my gratitude to the Educational Testing Service of Princeton, New Jersey, and the Russell Sage Foundation for kindly consenting to my use of the Ayres list of words from the AYRES MEASURING SCALE FOR ABILITY IN SPELLING.

Acknowledgment is also due the grateful parents of the hundreds of children with reading troubles whom I have taught individually. These parents have in large measure inspired me to put my teaching into book form. Perhaps I owe a debt most of all to these hundreds of children and to those in my many classrooms. Every one of them has worked with me, used his mind—and shown me just how it is that children learn to comprehend and use the written and spoken language.

This new edition is a revision, not because the first version written four years ago requires correction—that book is entirely true and right—but because certain arguments and statistics are no longer needed. Today most educators and reading textbook publishers and their writers and lecturers have discovered the inability of many, if not most, children to learn to read adequately without *some* attention to phonics, at least as a supplementary aid to whole-word reading.

What we *now* want to make clear is the practical impossibility of a classroom teacher's successfully teaching a mixture of the two methods—and the fallacy of the current claim by many elementary-school educators that some children learn best by one method and some by the other.

We have also elaborated on a few of the teaching techniques and added a few helpful ideas for classroom teaching and, in an appendix, a condensed teacher's guide or manual. These should enable the teacher to follow the book closely and at the same time more easily in her day-to-day work.

What this book offers is a full, accurate and clear working textbook for teachers and teachers' colleges to meet the fast growing demand for more phonics in elementary education. This is, I am sure, a great and much needed improvement in basic education.

This book is written for teachers and parents and so avoids technical terminology and pedantic phraseology. But the years of study, experiment and experience which created this teaching method are believed to provide the most nearly complete and accurate, practical presentation of phonics for teaching English. It is apparent that, aside from teaching the children, it also makes the written English language far more simple and logical and easier to learn and understand by foreign students of English. This can be a most important contribution.

THE WRITING ROAD TO READING

CHAPTER I

Changing Methods of Teaching the Language

THE CHILD, or the adult, who cannot easily read *and write* better English with a larger vocabulary than he normally uses in speaking, badly needs better teaching. Of course, this cannot apply to six-year-olds in their first year of school, but the groundwork for their facility with language should be laid in that first year. Many American first-grade teachers today would not concur with my conviction that every six-year-old who is sufficiently normal to be admitted to a school classroom is both willing and able to learn to read, write and spell. It is only true, in fact, when a simple, direct, logical and accurate method of teaching the language is used. The aim of this book is to provide just that. This book offers in the Unified Phonics Method an entirely different, but thoroughly tested approach to a phonics method of teaching writing, spelling and reading derived from accurate speaking.

Nothing in education is more vital to the future of America than that *all* its children shall learn to read and write easily, rapidly, accurately and enjoyably. A man who is not fairly well read in these changing times cannot pull his weight and be a competent member of our democracy. Everyone will agree that reading and writing ability is fundamental to every branch of education, and especially to self-education, all through life.

The Unified Phonics Method is one of learning by reasoning, rather than by memorizing alone. It comes at a time when a great many parents, and the American public generally, are justly alarmed at the failure of the schools to teach adequately the reading, writing, spelling and speaking of English to a high percentage of their children. Indeed, who cannot call to mind intelligent boys or girls who have been unable to get a complete education because of a lack of facility with the basic tools of learning? Who cannot think of someone whose normal ambitions have been impeded simply because he or she did not learn to read or write competently in elementary school?

Certainly it is not fair to look on non-readers or retarded readers as potential juvenile delinquents; yet we must recognize failure in school as a contributory cause of delinquency. The seeds of frustration and insecurity are sown too often in the elementary grades by failure to master reading and writing, and the unhappy, brooding child seeks an escape. To compensate for his failure, a child often becomes a bully or a truant, acquires hostility, or moves toward open rebellion, all of which can point in the dangerous direction of delinquency. The larger number who fail become shy and withdraw from every situation which might expose their weakness. As the happy, secure child is seldom a problem, we must strive in every way to make each child as free from failure as possible.

Any human situation is necessarily complex, and the factors affecting it are not always easy to isolate. Nonetheless, it must be said that the presence in our schools of an unhealthy percentage of retarded readers is due in large measure to reliance upon the so-called "sight or whole-word method" as the only technique sanctioned by most educators for the teaching of beginning reading. Its ascendancy came about in a rather strange way.

After the turn of the century many elementary school educators were influenced by the pragmatic philosophies of Dr. John Dewey of Columbia University. Dr. Dewey revolted against abstract learning; he thought of education as a tool which should enable an individual to integrate his culture and his vocation effectively. His contribution to the progressive school movement has won world-wide recognition, and his influence has been a strong factor in turning from the former reliance upon authoritarian methods toward the increasing emphasis upon learning through practice and experimentation. But in their zeal to apply Dr. Dewey's theories and to change old ways of teaching for interesting new ways in the 1920's, educators, in general, went overboard in making radical changes in the method of teaching reading and spelling.

It is true that the old pre-progressive way of teaching these subjects by phonics was neither scientific nor complete, and it was encumbered by tedious, ineffective drills. However, instead of the obvious faults being corrected, the whole phonics system was discarded and the sight method adopted. Before long most schools were attempting to teach children literally to memorize the *appearance* of every word, without the slightest regard for the sounds which the letters in sequence were meant to convey. In short, that great invention of the early Phoenicians, the letters of the alphabet as the symbols for sounds, was practically forsaken.

The chief method of teaching reading in the American schools is still the "whole-word recognition" or "sight" method as distinguished from the "sound" or phonics method. There are only these two, though educators often speak of there being many. To justify this statement I point out that Unified Phonics includes all the known, direct, means of teaching reading except that of memorizing the configuration or appearance of the "whole-word." The context is used to check on the phonetic analysis of a new word, and "structural analysis" is phonics applied to prefixes and endings of base words. The meaning of a word must be taught in either method, independently of the means by which the word is identified or recognized in print.

There are some children who learn to read very well, even to spell fairly well, under the sight method of teaching. These children, often numbering between one quarter and one third of a class, are those who are blessed with an excellent visual memory. In time they discover for themselves some of the connections between the letters and the sounds. Thus they derive a sort of homemade phonics, and the success of this fraction of the total number of pupils partly explains the confidence of many able teachers in the whole-word method.

But success for a minority is neither efficient nor half enough.

Between the two World Wars this so-called "whole-word" or sight method of teaching reading and spelling was uniformly required by American teachers' colleges as the one and only method permissible. No teaching certificate was possible if an applicant had not earned passing grades in this one method. It soon produced, however, such an alarming percentage of non-readers and very poor readers in American schools that a few years ago parents and university faculties all across the country began making strong protests. These criticisms within the last five years have reached such a volume and are so well founded on fact that most of the reading experts are now advocating that the method be supplemented later, after a beginning with sight reading, with more and more phonics teaching.

This is a great change, but the gain is limited indeed, and still leaves much to be desired from the standpoint of teaching all first-year children to read and write.

The idea is based upon a fallacy which is now widely accepted as true by all those who have heavy investments in the basal readers that start with the whole-word teaching. The fallacy is that some children's minds learn to read and write quite differently from those of others. Therefore they say the schools must teach some children by phonics and some by the whole-word method. They also contend that all need to *begin* learning by the whole-word method.

It is safe to say that most school officials now assert that their schools teach all methods. Unfortunately however, very, very few teachers today know enough about phonics to teach it accurately. Very few teachers' colleges in the country give a separate, full course in phonics. One reading of this book will make clear that a teacher does need to study and *learn* phonics thoroughly before teaching it.

The main reason why this idea of teaching all methods in a

schoolroom can be called a fallacious theory is that in practice it does not work with children. For them, guessing at an unfamiliar word by using any word that might fit into the sentence context, or trying to remember the word from its whole general appearance, takes less mental effort than analyzing the sounds of its component letters. This is even more true when the child has only a sketchy, incomplete knowledge of the phonograms. Perhaps the greatest harm done in teaching only the sight or whole-word method at the beginning is that it inculcates a bad mental habit towards all study at the very beginning of school, in the impressionable first months. Instead of being given certain basic tools with which to attack the reading or writing of words, by reasoning, by using his mind, as he must with phonics, the child is taught to guess at the words if his memory of its general appearance fails him. His first idea about studying is not thinking, but merely memorizing. It may take years to correct this.

There are also a majority in every class who have, to a greater or a less degree, a natural tendency to reverse, or confuse, the left-to-right sequence of letters. Phonics are absolutely essential to writing, spelling and reading for these children, and, in fact, phonics exactly as taught by the Unified Phonics Method—that is, beginning with the writing of the dictated phonograms. A child can never know the phonogram sounds without thorough basic instruction by a teacher who has a good knowledge of phonics herself. It is too much to expect that a teacher can be proficient and enthusiastic in two distinct and almost opposite approaches to the teaching of reading. They simply do not fit together. Thus, a dash of phonics teaching combined with the whole-word guessing method often serves only to confuse. The child resorts to guessing unless he has a real command of the tool of phonics, and guessing is easier. His whole attitude toward study is damaged because he abandons reasoning for either rote memorizing or mere guessing. It is imperative that he start with phonics. Sight reading then follows automatically.

Jacques Maritain, in his Terry lectures at Yale on the subject, "Education at the Crossroads," stated that what is learned should never be mechanically received as dead information but must be transformed by understanding into the very life of the mind. Reason which receives knowledge in a servile manner does not really know and is only depressed by a knowledge which is not its own, but that of others. On the contrary, reason which assimilates knowledge vitally —that is, in a free, liberating manner—really knows and is exalted by this knowledge, which henceforth is its own. Then it is that reason really masters the things learned.

When a six-year-old child is introduced to the written language, he already has acquired a speaking vocabulary of several thousand words. He, therefore, finds it novel and exciting to learn through phonics teaching to make certain characters on paper express the same sounds he uses in the words he knows. In manuscript writing these letters are almost identical with those he sees on the printed page. The whole vast world of letters thus makes sense to him. It is logical and understandable to him if *from the first* he is taught to write down the letters which express the sounds he speaks—that is, if he spells the words by writing their *sounds*. Reading those words follows almost automatically. He uses reasoning rather than pure rote memorizing in both his spelling and reading. His learning becomes an exciting, challenging experience.

In contrast to undisciplined restlessness of the average class during a lesson in sight reading, a class taught by this phonics method is quiet, keenly interested, concentrating on learning and working. The difference is so great it must be seen to be believed.

And even if the logic of this natural approach to reading were less apparent, perhaps it would be necessary only to cite the extent of the English vocabulary to prove the point.

Otto Jespersen, the Danish philologist who made brilliant contributions to the study of phonetics, the English language and linguistics in general, conducted an investigation on this subject many years ago. He studied a group of college students and found that the majority possessed reading vocabularies of a little less than 60,000 words. It is obvious that no one can begin to memorize the printed appearance of any such number. If, however, he has a basic grasp of phonics then each printed word automatically sounds in his mind at a glance. It speaks out to him instantly and clearly.

It is this simple and readily learned instrument which phonics provides, and with it completely at his command, almost any child can, by himself, learn to read anything written within the speaking vocabulary which he understands. This ability to read opens up to his eager imagination so many enthralling story books that from then on he seldom needs to be taught reading. He teaches himself. Very soon he recognizes at a glance, without recourse to his phonic knowledge, the short words and those which recur often. He soon reads such words by sight alone. He reserves his phonics knowledge for the printed words that are new to him, and he eventually comes to use it almost unconsciously, instantly, habitually. It does not impede his attention to the meaning of the word, or of the sentence. Instead it seems to eliminate any pondering or guessing at the word, thus simplifying and expediting the continuity of his comprehension of the whole sentence.

In the nature of things every growing child first acquires a speaking vocabulary. He should then learn handwriting, and simultaneously he should be taught how to translate the spoken sounds into the written symbols (namely, the phonograms) which represent them. By assembling these symbols into words he can write ideas, and inversely he can read his own or the ideas of others. This was the sequence which the human race followed in building its alphabetic languages.

It is fundamental and logical that from the beginning the child should learn thoroughly the relation between the sounds of speech and their written symbols, for reading is not "guessing" at the meaning of words. It is not getting the meaning of a word by looking at an adjacent picture illustrating the word. It is not even pronouncing the sounds in sequence of the phonograms which constitute the spelling of the word. And reading is *not* getting the idea by having teacher tell what the word says. Reading is rather the process whereby the reader remembers those words he has often read before and mentally translates into sound the new words he encounters. He thereby instantly recognizes them, and their meaning falls into place among the other words he already knew. His mind then weighs the import of the sentence, for judgment is a vital part of reading.

The common misunderstanding about the phonetic basis of English and how it should be taught accounts for the claim that phonics teaching tends to block a child's easy comprehension in reading. In fact it appears that scientific and true phonics teaching eliminates the blocking of the reader's comprehension. When he must otherwise search his memory to recall the word by its overall appearance or, that failing, must just guess at it, then he does tend to lose the meaning of the sentence. If each difficult word is accompanied by an illustrative cartoon he gets a rough idea of what the word says from the picture. But that is not reading English. It is more like puzzling through a "comic" strip.

The Unified Phonics Method is distinctly different and its supplies what has been lacking heretofore—a simple, workable and thorough method for teaching phonics in the home or in the classroom. This method differs basically from other phonic methods in that it does not start with reading, which is, in phonics, the translating of printed letters or words into the sounds of spoken words. It avoids the use of charts, trick gadgets or other expensive devices. Instead it first teaches the child the *writing* of the sounds by using the letters which say the sounds. This direct approach from the *sounds* of the words the child knows and uses in speaking into the *written characters* which represent the sounds is a direct, simple, logical explanation to him of the whole writing and reading process. He is not bewildered by this new world of letters. He grasps the idea almost at once. He is delighted to find that he can use the twenty-six letters of the alphabet to say on paper the many words he speaks. In other words, he learns to spell. As soon as he can write a word he can usually read it, often at a glance wherever he sees it. In fact, reading as such need not be taught to many children, but training in the *blending* of the sounds in a syllable is needed for some. When a child has once mastered the phonic tools, he is able to decipher and pronounce and understand any printed words which come within his speaking vocabulary. Not only does he comprehend those words but also the many others which he hears and understands, but has not as yet come to use.

The fact that this method teaches spelling first, by actually writing the sounds of words on paper, is believed to be a complete departure from other phonics teaching methods, and a distinct advance. The other major contribution is the completeness of its phonetics, and its simplicity. There is a reason or rule to cover *almost* every spelling in English. A study of word formation and euphony has contributed to formulating a set of easily learned, simple rules which explain and govern the spelling of most words.

I have called this system of teaching the language subjects the Unified Phonics Method because it is based on showing and teaching the constant connection between the sounds of the spoken language and the characters which represent them in the written language. Speaking, writing, spelling and reading are taught as related parts of a single subject—the English language—and the method follows the same natural teaching sequence by which man developed language itself. Furthermore it is based on the physical and neurological processes of the human brain. It is also carefully designed to prevent the typical errors which children make in speech, spelling and reading. In a word it is a scientific method of teaching language.

All of us do use word recognition in reading. We must acquire it, and after learning phonics we do so almost automatically, often without any teaching or training, and in accordance with the acuity of our individual visual memories. Sight reading or recogniton of words at a glance requires no teaching for a child who knows phonics. Common and familiar words are soon recognized and read at sight with easy sentence comprehension *provided* the tool of phonics is at hand to indentify any new or less familiar words. However it has been found to be very confusing to the great majority of first- or second-grade children who are taught this method if any form of whole word recognition, or sight method of teaching is introduced.

These are the children who are not born with "unilateral dominance" for reading, but have to acquire it. Unilateral dominance is an inherited physical characteristic which has no relation to intelligence. It is, in effect, as Dr. Orton demonstrated, the mental habit of always using the same side of the brain to receive and retain the image of printed letters in words for the purpose of fixing meaning to them. This habit results in the image always showing in one drection. However, most children inherit more or less of a tendency to use either side of the brain, a tendency which results in their sometimes receiving the image of the letters in reverse, or more often in the image being confused. These latter children comprise at least half of any group, and usually three-fourths of the boys. The extent of their resultant reading disability varies all the way from an easily corrected degree for some children to a complete disability for others when any sight reading is attempted.

The Spalding method corrects the chief defect in the whole-word method of teaching. This major defect is that no cure is provided for the normal child who often reverses or confuses the left-to-right sequence of the printed letters he sees. This tendency exists, I repeat, to a greater or less serious degree in most children.

For many years I have tested individually children who have serious language disabilities—probably close to three thousand of them. Something like 95 per cent have clearly shown this reversal or confusion. It is the basic cause of their problem in reading and spelling. I know this because nearly all have gone to tutors trained in my method and have learned to overcome their language failures. That is one of the main reasons we start, not by reading, but by writing the phonograms and words from the teacher's verbal dictation. The children repeat these aloud just before writing each one. This training for such children reinforces the left-to-right sequence through four channels, hearing it, feeling it in the muscles of the mouth and of the hand, and seeing it as they write it. Dr. Samuel Orton used this procedure successfully to teach children who were by other methods serious reading failures.

The Spalding method of unified phonics is a development from this same technique. It is the method whereby *all* children in a group, even those who inherit the above handicap in severe form, can be taught to master the English language through *writing* the sounds from the start of schooling. It prevents non-readers. It eliminates the present great need for "remedial reading" in later years.

Thus, the method is very much more than a complete and accurate system of phonics teaching. It is that, but it also teaches correct speech, writing, and spelling and a classroom technique for the early prevention of language failures of elementary children in large classes.

School administrators and teachers who wish to try out the Unified Phonics Method are often confronted by a problem as to what policy to follow when it is not practical to begin it in all classes in the school. I can report on how this has worked out in some schools. After three or four months of Unified Phonics teaching, even in one classroom, its advantages became apparent. Other teachers became interested. They studied the book and formed a group for a course taught by one of the experienced teachers. Thus it soon spread through the school. The problem is solved by the interest aroused in the method due to its success in actual use. Many teachers have done very well with nothing except this book as a guide for teaching. The book is intended to give all the instruction and techniques which are needed, but the training in a forty-hour study course is desirable.

The question naturally arises also as to the effect on children who are taught by one method in one grade and by another in their next grade. Does the change confuse or block their progress in language? Evidently not in practice. Children who have had sight-method teaching in their first year or two years, have to start in phonics from the beginning, but after a few weeks most can progress at a faster rate than those in first grade. On the other hand those who have had Unified Phonics from the start, or even for one year, and are then placed with a sight-method teacher seem not to lose their ability to apply phonics knowledge.

The Unified Phonics Method of teaching enables every child in a group to acquire the habit of left to right sequence as is necessary for reading without delaying or disturbing the progress of those fortunate few who easily acquire it. As in the teaching of any subject, some children need much more time and attention than others. This training in left to right sequence is where parents can be of enormous help because they can learn and teach the Unified Phonics Method at home without interfering with, but actually supplementing and reinforcing the classroom teaching.

It seems essential, in fact, that parents as well as teachers should know and understand the methods of teaching the English language to children. Education cannot be confined to the classroom. Most children want to be shown how to write and to read long before they reach school age. There is every reason why they should be taught as many of the preliminary steps at home as they can master, provided the right method is used.

CHAPTER II

Experience with the Unified Phonics Method

SCIENTIFICALLY VALID experiments to show the relative values of different methods of teaching reading are most difficult to achieve. This is because it is almost impossible to set up reasonably similar conditions in two groups of classrooms for trials of two methods during a sufficient length of time—say, four years. Perhaps 120 children in each group of classes would suffice; but in each class the average I.Q., age, home living conditions and similar factors affecting the pupils' capacity to learn, and likewise the several teachers' education, enthusiasm, good health and quality, should all be equated if the test scores in the end are to be acceptable as a true measure of each method. Even if it were possible to begin a large enough experiment with all these factors almost in balance, the passage of time is certain to unbalance some of them.

The one valid test—the true comparison between methods of teaching—is the actual experience of every teacher who has learned and taught the Unified Phonics Method in regular classrooms after having formerly taught similar classes by any other method. The following quotations are typical of expressions from school heads and teachers who are experienced both with the Unified Phonics Method and with other methods of teaching reading. It is important to say that I have received hundreds of such enthusiastic reports of favorable experiences in teaching this method, favorable without reservations other than that the teacher needs to study and to work at it.

A large parochial school in Hawaii has used this method for the past six years in all grades from kindergarten to the ninth. There are today 790 children in sixteen classrooms. The children are not tested for their I.Q. or otherwise for admission to kindergarten and first grade. The school has an enviable reputation. The reason is that despite an average of fifty children per classroom in the primary grades, every child learns by the Spalding method to read, write and spell. Many first-graders read third-grade library books, but even the slowest read fully up to their grade level. The spirit of interest and success in the language studies on the part of the whole school can only be appreciated by experiencing it.

The principal of this school writes:

Bright children go forward at an amazing pace into the world of books. The method does its work surely and quickly for this type of child. Their independence in attacking new words and their freedom from the slavery of remembering the countless words of our language stimulate their desire to achieve . . .

Slower children are none the less benefited. These children go through a similar development but at their own rate of achievement. The method is ideally geared to the indivuality of the child, to his slower learning ability.

He masters a definite number of phonograms at his own pace. The emotional upset and frustration of trying to recall hundreds of sight words is avoided. The seeing, saying and writing of the sounds simultaneously eliminates some of the slow child's biggest reading pitfalls, such as reversals, poor auditory discrimination, inability to follow directions, and general habits of inattention.

I have dwelt at length on the beginnings, but here, as in every worthwhile undertaking, beginnings count double. Our beginnings, thanks to the Unified Phonic Method approach to the Language Arts, have counted for double or more. We have a small quota of slow readers, but not one non-reader. Our slow readers are in fact a definite proof of the genuineness and complete reliability of the method. These readers are slow, but they are *always progressing*. Our classroom records show steady, even daily reading progress for all our children of low average or very low mental ability.

An overall proof of the excellent results of using this method over a period of seven years is the reading consciousness throughout the school and the consistent scholastic achievement. Because the pupils can read, teachers have been able to take the time to guide them into important phases of comprehension and into the intellectual wealth of the literature of the language. Reading can be directed, individualized, and made the gateway to knowledge and wisdom.

The Unified Phonic Method requires from the teacher dedication and hard work. If a teacher is seeking an easy way of teaching, let her look elsewhere—it is not here. If she is seeking a sure way, let her look into this method with an open mind and a real desire to know. If she is seeking a way to guide children through reading to well adjusted personality, this method will not fail her.

Through the use of this method in our school we have had the satisfaction of seeing very large classes of children well started in reading, adventuring on their own and achieving in general scholastic work. In fine we have experienced the joy of a difficult task well done.

The superintendent of twenty-four Catholic schools in Hawaii expressed his attitude toward this method thus:

This approach to the comprehensive mastery of language is the only logical one. It comes to grips immediately with the symbolic character of the spoken and written word and shows the inter-relationship of the two symbol systems and their power to evoke common meanings.

Pupils, too, are quick to feel a sense of satisfaction in the "workableness" of the approach. They gain a healthy independence from the teacher and all extrinsic aids. Once the tools of learning are mastered the way to learning lies open. If some children seem to master the tools of language effortlessly and without the need for method, still many do not. Furthermore, it cannot be denied that whatever the ability of the pupil, this is a systematic and scientific way to lead him to language facility.

The principal of a private school in Honolulu says:

With regard to the use of your approach to reading in Epiphany School, we feel entirely at a loss for words to express how great this contribution has been.

When I look back at our struggles in trying to help children to read by the picture-sight method and the frustration we saw in the children together with the countless wasted hours, it is hard to realize that this situation could ever have existed.

Last year I made a thorough check on reading ability at each grade level and in each case I found one-third of the class reading at grade level, one-third reading a year in advance and one-third reading two or more grade levels above. Perhaps it is also important to add that with your system we have no one reading below grade level and no one who has serious reading difficulties; although we frequently have in the group reading on grade level pupils who need more attention because of lack of maturity or lack of inclination to work.

The principal of the lower school in a leading private school at Houston, Texas, says:

Speaking for one of the independent schools using this method, we are delighted. Our children are writing more legibly, spelling better and reading earlier. Several fathers have stated that this method uses an intellectual process with logical thinking as the result.

From another private school in Houston the principal writes:

Now I am glad to say we have used the Spalding method for one year, and are remarkably impressed with the uniform success it has wrought with our students.

We have a first grade which scores a median of 3.8 on spelling, with individual scores as high as 5.0, and none scoring less than 3.1. Our second grade read at a median of 3.9 after eight months, and spelled at 4.6. Grade five completed eight months reading at a 7.5 median, with individuals reading as high as 10.3. Problem readers, readers with deeply embedded problems, gained as much as 3½ years within eight months. One of these gained two of the years after mid-term, and others without reading problems gained more. It proved to be the incentive for accelerated readers, spellers, and writers, but it proved the same for the ordinary and for the one with serious deficiencies.

We found great improvement in comprehension, for they knew the background of words, and cared much more about the language, as well as the proper use for it.

One of our teachers has just finished a week of teaching the course eight hours a day to some sixty teachers. Among them were two teachers who had heard Mrs. Spalding last year and had followed her instructions completely, and kept records of it all. They are delighted to sit through it again, and their praise is the very highest.

The principal of a public School in Oberlin, Ohio, says:

The classroom atmosphere in the rooms where this method is being used is conspicuous for the enthusiasm of the children and the teacher, and the fact that the less capable children take to it with the same zeal as the more capable. They like it because they experience success.

An eminent professor of psychology at Oberlin College has looked into this method and has this to say:

What pleases me most is the way this method gets across from reading with the ear to reading with the eye. When a child comes to school he has been "reading" with his ear for years—really a very complex skill.

Mrs. Spalding's method is so good because it takes the sound which comes into his ear, and which he repeats in his own speech (and thus hears again), and teaches him to write the visual symbol for this sound, *which he sees because he made it*. Because his muscles are involved in making the correctly oriented movement, his eyes are trained in the proper orientation habits necessary for reading. This is the way to prevent reversals so common in children taught by the sight method. Teaching reading is actually a good deal easier than teachers have thought it was. What they have lacked was a proper teaching method.

An experienced teacher of large first-grade classes in another Honolulu parochial school writes:

A phonics method to be worthy of that title must be simple enough for the youngest or poorest of the pupils to grasp, yet broad enough in its scope to provide the "attack readiness" for all words. Because of the method, every word should be familiar to the child; familiar in the sense that, when confronted with a "new" word, he will be able to master it, *not* in relation to another word, but solely by intellectually "sounding it out". The Spalding method can fulfill these requirements. It provides the child with a simple, logical, yet comprehensive tool, which when acquired, enables him to attack any word phonetically constructed. Its difficult aspect (which is far from insurmountable) is in the mastering of the sounds and the rules governing the sounds. What the child gains is the knowledge and facility necessary for adult reading and correct spelling. And that is no small asset.

A teacher long experienced in the primary department of another Hawaii school remarks that:

One of the outstanding features of this method is its organization. There may be other methods of teaching phonics, but, I am sure, none that are more highly organized or logically developed.

Does it lead to "word" reading? The only children that may come in this category are those who have to "sound out" before they can recognize the word, but these are the children who would not be able to read at all, ordinarily. The sense of confidence that they develop in knowing that they can attack a word soon leads to smooth reading. The other children progress as rapidly as they can and are able to enjoy an enriched education because they no longer must "wait" until the word is presented to them.

There has been a definite influence on other subject matter also. This method develops an alertness and conscious intellectualization that carries over into other subjects. The relationship between the spoken word and the written word is in itself the key to this method and this habit of accurate speaking and writing is a real aid to clear thinking.

One final remark concerns the result of this method on Parents, Child and Teacher. Once they realize the value of this method the parents are 100 per cent in favor of it. If they wish to assist their child there is a text available by which they can contribute to his progress by using the same method that the teacher is using.

A third-grade teacher in Oberlin, Ohio, writes:

"No method, that I know, is as basic and searching in its approach to the problems of reading and spelling as the Spalding Unified Phonics."

The headmaster of a school in Weston, Massachusetts, writes:

We have incorporated your *The Writing Road to Reading* in the kindergarten through sixth grade here. All the teachers enjoy it very much, and our first- and second-grade teachers are extremely enthusiastic about it.

This fall we had a workshop in which all of us read your book through orally and listened to your phonograms which you made on tape at Peterborough.

The following recent report is from the principal of a public school near Los Angeles:

In grades two through six the children who were in classes that did not use the phonics approach showed an average increase in spelling ability of six months during seven months of instruction. In the fourteen classes using the Unified Phonics, the average increase was fourteen months during seven months of instruction. It should be mentioned that two of the classes not included in the Unified Phonics group were taught by teachers who emphasize phonics in their teaching. These classes were higher on the average than the regular classes but still below those who used the new method.

It should be emphasized that although these figures are very impressive, all of the children who had reading problems (it was shown they also had spelling problems) and were achieving less than a year for each year spent in school, were placed in the classes using Unified Phonics. Those who were outstanding readers and spellers, with the exception of the second grade, were placed in classes using the regular method.

All teachers and children were and are enthusiastic over the Unified Phonics approach to the language arts.

Although there are not test results to show the progress made in reading, handwriting, language and composition, all of the teachers have expressed enthusiasm over the obvious improvement in these areas as well.

Of the eight teachers who were unable to attend the workshop last summer, seven plan to take it this summer if they are placed where they may teach it next year.

A first-grade public-school teacher in Fairbanks, Alaska, who learned the method solely by studying the book, had this to say in reporting to the superintendent last summer:

In September, 32 first-graders chosen on the basis of permanent residence only, were started in a reading program using the Unified Phonics approach.

We can now report the following results:

As a whole, the thirty-two first-graders have made very good progress. They have maintained a high level of interest, acquired good work habits and developed independence and self-confidence.

Ten pupils are capable of reading material of fifth- and sixth-grade level of difficulty. These children read second- and third-grade material with ease and fluency.

Ten pupils achieved at a somewhat lower level but are capable of reading third- and fourth-grade material, and read first- and second-grade material with ease and fluency.

The next seven pupils are well prepared for second grade, reading primer and first-grade material well. Since they are not limited to the vocabulary of one reading series, they are more independent than most average first-graders.

Of the remaining five children, four are reading primer material and can spell many words.

The test showed one very interesting fact: the method used in the experimental program seemed particularly beneficial for boys. 60 per cent of the boys in group X ranked in the upper quartile of the distribution as compared to 11 per cent of the boys in the non-experimental group.

The above quotations were selected as showing various aspects of the method as it has worked out in classroom use in widely separated American schools.

There are today a number of other well-known methods of teaching reading by phonics. None of them, I believe, depend on the teaching of accurate speech, writing and spelling along with the reading, as does Unified Phonics. However, I think that any method of teaching phonics is better than none and definitely tends to improve a child's ability in reading.

It is my belief, based on many years of continuous observation and teaching experience, that it is better not to use any form of games, or play, in teaching the written language to children. It is best to teach them to use their minds not only for amusement, but for work. Neither pictures nor fanciful phrasing of spelling rules nor anything but the most direct and simple teaching of these rules and the phonogram sounds is desirable. I have found that extraneous ideas interfere with the direct, easy learning and use of the spelling rules and the phonogram sounds. I even use the sounds of the letters, wherever possible, instead of their names for that same reason. Young children are so eager to read and so entranced with the ability to put into writing the words and sounds they use in speaking that the straight business of teaching and working at it holds their complete attention.

There are some important objectives and reasons for these techniques. They are not all found in other methods and, before one goes into the detail of the method, they should be understood.

My approach to all words is by phonics. This full understading of a word is the most certain way of placing it securely in the child's sight vocabulary. One other important reason for this approach is to build the mental habit of thinking—of applying the child's knowledge of phonics to the attack of a new word, rather than for him to guess at it from the context or from pictures. It is this new habit of reasoning, of applying what he has learned, to solve each word problem that is so valuable for his mental growth. It builds sound future study habits right from the beginning. The child acquires the right attitude of mind towards all his school work.

Another very important objective of this method relates to the fact, already referred to, that in any class a large percentage of the children inherit a tendency sometimes to reverse or to confuse the sequence of letters in a word. This tendency is entirely independent of a child's intelligence. If this is caught early before habits are fixed, it can soon be corrected. That is one reason I start at the beginning to teach writing from the spoken word. It establishes the mental habit of the left-to-right sequence. The child hears the word and says each syllable aloud just before he writes it and then reads the whole word aloud. Thus the proper sequence of phonograms in the word is fixed by his hearing it, saying it with his mouth, writing it with his hand and seeing it with his eye. For very many children, and especially for boys, this beginning training is of vital importance. Suffice it to say that by this simple means we can eliminate nearly all remedial reading problems from the first grade upwards. In all confusion cases we try to teach parents enough so that they can understand and help the child at home.

Many years of continuous teaching in this method have enabled me to refine it in every detail, so as to avoid every element in teaching technique which might create an obstacle to a child's learning well and rapidly. Many of these obstacles are suprisingly minor items. One major obstacle is handwriting, so I have developed an exact but simple and workable set of techniques for forming the manuscript letters and, later on, the connected writing. Facility in writing is a great and basic help in learning to spell and read.

Another necessary ability in learning by phonics is the correct pronunciation of words. This not only makes the writing and reading more accurate; it is a direct gain in teaching the habit of accurate, clear speech. That, of course for anyone who knows his phonograms, makes English spelling much easier to master. With these matters well learned much less teaching time is needed on the mechanics of teaching reading. We do very much *oral* reading in the reading period and very early turn to stories, or whole books, which have true literary merit. We discuss and analyze any new words just as they happen to come up in a story, not separately, after a fair vocabulary has been acquired from the study of the Ayres-list words.

CHAPTER III

Fundamentals in Teaching Phonics

THE WRITTEN or printed language should be presented to a beginner as a series of symbols each of which represents one of the component sounds of a spoken word. This is fundamental. It ties together logically the written and the spoken word. Speaking, writing and reading are thus understood and taught as related. This is the only reasoned approach to any alphabetic language.

There are 70 common phonograms in English. They are the single letters or letter combinations which represent 45 *basic* sounds used in the spoken language. (The phonograms are listed at the end of this chapter.) The first step in reading and spelling is to learn these phonograms so well that in any printed word they stand out clearly *as a series of sounds*, and not merely as a series of letters.

The short and common words soon come to be recognized automatically as representing ideas, without the need of separating them into their component phonograms for reading. Writing at first requires such analysis to get the spelling right. For spelling, new words should always be studied by their phonetic sounds from the *spoken* word. True spelling is writing from the spoken word.

I have found that it is a mistake to place spelling books in the hands of the children. "Spelling" books are not good for teaching

37

spelling because they do not help to relate the spelling to the sounds of the words. If the child looks at printed words and merely copies them, he learns only by memory and without reasoning. Few spelling books tell the child to translate any of the letters into their corresponding sounds. They make him depend almost wholly on his visual recall. This is a real handicap to most if not to all children. I repeat, true spelling is translating *speech* into written symbols.

Most spelling books now introduce new words in whole sentences or paragraphs, but that makes it a reading, not a spelling, lesson.

In teaching spelling by the Unified Phonics Method new words are dictated by the teacher and written by the children from her verbal dictation. Any troublesome words are discussed from the point of view of the symbols which represent the sounds. The spelling is first reasoned, then memorized. The meaning is of course discussed. "Word" connotes meaning. A word is the smallest unit of speech which by itself has any meaning. The children give oral sentences containing the new word. Then, assuming he has a sufficient vocabulary, each child writes *his own* original sentence containing it. This teaches true *spelling* in the spelling lesson.

The spelling lesson is where we teach the relationship between the spoken and written word. That is why in spelling we use the numbers and underlinings of certain phonograms to identify which sound, or which spelling of a sound, is used in each part of the word wherever more than one is possible. These markings make the child *think* about which is used and why. They help very much in fixing these important details in his mind. The details of these markings are given on pages 128 and 129.

We do not use the shortened spellings which the dictionary uses to show the pronunciation of words—simply because this confuses and leads to misspellings. With our markings it is unnecessary—is, in fact, a deterrent to normal spelling. As soon as a child can read he should learn to use the dictionary for definitions of meanings. Then, after he has learned a good vocabulary and correct pronunciation, but not before, he should be taught the system of markings used in the dictionary for pronouncing words. It is, I believe, a serious error to introduce any of the international phonetic markings or sounds until a child in the upper grades seriously studies a foreign language. Speed reading also should not be introduced until a child has mastered the basic and accurate speaking, writing and reading of the language.

I should like to point out that this method requires of both teacher and pupil accurate pronunciation of the language. It clarifies the sounds for children as nothing else can. It will, I hope, help upgrade the present tendency toward the slovenly and deteriorated speaking of our language. The vowel sounds in non-accented syllables should not sound like the slovenly "uh" and most of these should be thought of just as they are spelled. However, the precise sound is lost, to some extent, in the natural rhythm of English speech.

A suggested teaching program or teacher's guide for her classroom use of this book has been outlined in the Appendix. It is important that, in using this guide, the teacher should not let it serve to slow down the progress of her class, nor of the more able children in the class. It is a mistake to place any brake on the advance of any child in the field of reading.

Two-thirds of the phonograms have only one sound. Eleven have two sounds and ten have three sounds. In addition to learning the phonograms, and applying them, there are a few laws of spelling which must be learned and used. All of them are summarized at the end of Chapter V.

The above may seem like a difficult project for a six-year-old; actually it is not. He learns both the phonograms and the laws rapidly and easily. They are simple and logical statements. The mental capacity of a six-year-old is not to be underestimated nor should his desire to learn be unrecognized.

Keeping this in mind, the teacher will see the importance of following exactly certain general procedures in her work. I have evolved these procedures by the most careful trial and testing over many years. These procedures, with neither additions nor deletions, I have found to be the most effective for successful results with all children.

First and foremost, the parent and teacher should elicit the intelligent and enthusiastic interest of the child in learning the written language. And this can only be done well by opening the door for him to the basis and meaning of writing—namely, that the letters stand for the sounds he makes when he says a word. Take any purely phonetic word, divide it verbally and in writing into syllables, and then divide the syllables into the phonetic sounds of each letter. Have him repeat the separate letter sounds (not their names), the syllables and the word. Tell him the letters *are* these sounds, not that they are merely symbolic of the sounds. And then explain that this is all there is to the written and printed words. Tell him you will teach him the sounds of the letters and how to write them, and that he can then write words and can say the words which others have written (or printed in books). This prospect is enough to excite the keenest interest of a child. The teaching procedures given below will maintain that same interest in the language subjects throughout his elementary school years.

One. Teach the phonograms by having the pupils say in unison the one or more sounds of each phonogram, showing them one phonogram card after another in varying sequences. Correct handwriting is taught from the very start, practicing only with the phonograms. Have them write on paper each phonogram just *after* they pronounce it. This unites the visual, aural and kinesthetic functions of the brain. The child sees, hears, says, writes and feels the symbol, and thus learns it. He is made aware of just how he makes the precise sounds, and of how he forms the related symbols for each phonogram.

Two. Avoid naming the letters. Use their phonetic sounds instead. The child should come to *think* of the letters as being sounds. (In English words, only five (ā, ē, ī, ō, ū) of the twenty-six letters *ever* use the sound of their names, and these five letters more often say ă, ĕ, ĭ, ŏ, ŭ). It is easier to unify speech, writing and reading by not injecting the names of letters. This simplifies the learning of the language. (Of course, before the third grade the children should know the name by which we designate the letter when talking of it, but the teaching time for spelling in all grades should be spent learning its sounds rather than its name.)

Three. Always call the phonogram containing two or more letters by its sound; that is to say, never spell it out. For example, eigh (which we call the four-letter "ā") has one sound. "Neighbor" contains four phonograms and "naval" contains five; the first five letters in "neighbor" have the same two sounds as the first two in "naval." The child should be taught to identify every phonogram in a word readily, and to think habitually of each as a distinct sound, whether it is a one-letter or a four-letter phonogram.

Four. Teach and require accurate pronunciation and correct, legible handwriting from the very beginning.

Five. As soon as the phonograms are fairly well learned, dictate words from the Ayres list for the children to write, making sure that they say aloud each phonogram of a one-syllable word and *each syllable* of longer words *just before* they start to write it. The children are not to see these words on the board or elsewhere, until they write them.

Six. Teach the basic laws (and exceptions) for spelling as they come up in writing words. The pupils should learn to use them by repeating the applicable spelling laws in every new word they write, until each child knows *and* uses them.

Seven. Where no rule governs the choice of which phonogram to use to represent a certain sound in a word, it can only be learned by memory, and the dictionary is referred to as the only authority. (We are not inventing a language; we are learning to understand and use the one we have.)

Eight. Remember that the real study of the language—the time when the pupils and teacher analyze the connection between the sound of a spoken word and its written symbols—is in the spelling period. Spelling is the basic key to a grasp of the written language and, for that matter, of the spoken one.

Nine. Reading from a book is not begun until the pupils have completely learned (just as outlined in the above procedures) enough common words to comprehend instantly the meaning of a sentence.

The phonograms are printed on the following pages. In teaching it is very convenient to use seventy separate cards which display the phonograms in type large enough to be seen across the room. The cards have the key sounds in smaller type printed on the back only for the teacher's information. The child learns only the sounds and the writing of them. Prove to him that these sounds are in the words he says, but do not teach the sounds by having him use key words.

The test of his knowledge of the sounds is shown by his ability to write the phonograms when only the sounds are given. For example, the teacher says, without showing the phonogram, the sound or sounds and the children write the phonogram.

It is important to follow all the teaching notes, the sequences, and the instructions given in this book. If this is done it is confidently predicted that a conscienticus teacher will have no normally intelligent child in her group below the national median level. Indeed, the median for the group should soon be about two years beyond the present national average in both reading and spelling, as well as in handwriting and speech.

Before teaching the sounds it is advisable to check and correct one's pronunciation of the phonograms. For example the sound of *l* is not "el" but only that of the last letter, the sound "b" is not "bŭh," and "k" is not "cŭh." We do not say robŭ but only rob. Segregate the phonogram sounds in the key words as a check on the correct sounds.

The 70 phonograms which follow were worked out by a group of language teachers under Dr. Samuel T. Orton's direction. They are also printed on separate cards with key words to show their one or more sounds printed on the reverse side of each just as shown here.

Boxed sets of single phonogram cards, 6″ x 4½″, are available as is a L.P. record of the presentation of the phonogram. For information and prices write to Whiteside, Inc., 425 Park Avenue South, New York 16, N. Y.

b

f

c

g

d

h

4

f

if

1

b

rib

5

g

"g"   bag

"j"   gem

g can say "j" only when followed by e, i or y. Thus the sound of this letter can be readily determined and no number is needed to indicate the use of the second sound.

2

c

"k"   can

"s"   cent

c followed by e, i or y says "s." Followed by any other letter it says "k." Thus the sound of this letter can be told at a glance so no number is needed to indicate the second sound.

6

h

him

3

d

lid

j	m
k	n
l	p

10

m

am

7

j

jam

11

n

in

8

k

ink

12

p

map

9

l

lag

"l" is sounded with the tongue point pressed against the roof of the mouth.

This is also true of "d," "t," and "n."

qu	t
r	v
s	w

16

t

bat

13

qu

"kw" quit

This sound is always written with two letters. The u is not a vowel here.

17

v

viv id

The teeth are placed on the lower lip at the same place for "f" as for "v." In writing many children confuse these two sounds unless they are taught to hear and feel the differences.

14

r

rat

"r" is sounded with the tongue point at the roof of the mouth. "r" is not "er."

18

w

wit

Round the lips to say "w." The sound is not "wŭ."

15

s

"s" us

"z" aš²

s never says "z" at the beginning of a base word: zoo, zebra, zero, etc.

x	a
y	e
z	i

22

a

"ă" at

"ā" na̱ vy

"ah" wȧnt

19

x

"ks" box

In "tacks" the "k" is a separate sound from the "s." Sound the "ks" of x as one sound.

23

e

"ĕ" end

"ē" me̱

20

y

yet

This consonant letter y is used only at the beginning of a syllable, usually the first one.

"ĭ" ba̱ by

"ī" my̱

24

i

"ĭ" In di an

"ī" si̱ lent

Both i's in Indian say "ĭ." i and y at the end of a syllable usually say "ĭ." The other vowels should say their names at the end of a syllable.

21

z

zest

o	ir
u	ur
er	wor

28	25
ir fi̲rst Her first nurse works early.	o "ŏ" odd "ō" o̲ pen "o͞o" do̤³
29	**26**
ur n̲u̲rse̲=⁵ Her first nurse works early.	u "ŭ" up "ū" mu̲² sic "o͝o" pṳt³
30	**27**
wor w̲o̲rks Her first nurse works early. (wor is made of two phonograms. or may say "er" when w comes before it.)	er he̲r Her first nurse works early. This sentence gives five spellings for the sound "er."

ear	th
sh	ay
ee	ai

34 ## th "th" <u>th</u>in (Breath hisses between tongue-tip and upper teeth) "t̶h̶"² <u>th</u>is (Tongue position is same as above but the voice gives sound as air is forced out)	**31** ear **<u>ear</u> ly** Her first nurse works early.
35 ay "ā" d<u>ay</u>	**32** ## sh **di<u>sh</u>** sh is used at the beginning of a word, at the end of a syllable, but not at the beginning of a syllable after the first one.
36 ai "ā" p<u>ai</u>nt	**33** ee "ē̄" s<u>ee</u>

ow	oi
ou	aw
oy	au

40 oi p<u>oi</u>nt	**37** ow "ow" h<u>ow</u> "$\bar{o}$" l<u>ow</u>²
41 aw l<u>aw</u>	**38** ou "ow" r<u>ou</u>nd "$\bar{o}$" f<u>ou</u>²r "$\bar{oo}$" y<u>ou</u>³ "$\breve{u}$" c<u>ou</u>⁴n try
42 au f<u>au</u>lt	**39** oy b<u>oy</u>

ew	ch
ui	ng
oo	ea

46 ch "ch" mu<u>ch</u> "k" s<u>ch</u>ool "sh" <u>ch</u>iv al ry	**43** ew "ōō" gr<u>ew</u> "ū" n<u>ew</u> (Same sounds as for ui.)
47 ng ra<u>ng</u> (ng is a nasal sound. It is neither "n" nor "g" nor is it a combination of them.)	**44** ui "ōō" fr<u>ui</u>t "ū" s<u>ui</u>t (Same sounds as for ew.)
48 ea "ē" <u>ea</u>t "ĕ" h<u>ea</u>d "ā" br<u>ea</u>k	**45** oo "ōō" b<u>oo</u>t "ŏŏ" f<u>oo</u>t "ō" fl<u>oo</u>r

ar	**or**
ck	**wh**
ed	**oa**

52	**49**
or	ar
<u>or</u>	f<u>ar</u>
53	**50**
wh	ck
"hw" <u>wh</u>en	ne<u>ck</u>
h is a breathing sound and therefore h + w is not the same sound as w alone.	(Used only after a single vowel which does not say its name.)
54	**51**
	ed
oa	"ĕd" grad <u>ed</u>
<u>boa</u>t	"d" love<u>d</u>²
	"t" <u>wr</u>ecke<u>d</u>³
	This card is the past tense ending—not the "ĕ" and "d" of red.

ey	igh
ei	eigh
ie	kn

62

58 igh "ī" s<u>igh</u>	**55** ey "ā" <u>they</u> [2] "ē" ke<u>y</u> [2] "ĭ" val l<u>ey</u> [3]
59 eigh "ā" w<u>eigh</u>	**56** ei "ē" con c<u>ei</u>t "ā" v<u>ei</u>l [2] "ĭ" for f<u>ei</u>t [3] See page 3 in the notebook for the rule for the use of ei and ie.
60 kn "n" <u>kn</u>ot Used only at the beginning of a base word.	**57** ie "ē" f<u>ie</u>ld "ī" p<u>ie</u> [2] "ĭ" lil <u>ies</u> [3][2] See page 3 in the notebook for the rule for the use of ie and ei.

gn

dge

wr

oe

ph

gh

64	**61**
dge	**gn**
"j" bridge	"n" gnat
May be used only after a single vowel which does not say its name.	Used both at the beginning and at the end of a base word. (reign)
65	**62**
oe	**wr**
"ō" toe	"r" wrap
	There is no sound of w here.
66	**63**
gh	**ph**
"g" ghost	"f" phan tom

ti	ough
si	
ci	

70

ough

"ō"   t̶hough²

"o͞o"   throu̇gh²

"ŭf"   rou̇gh³

"ŏf"   cou̇gh⁴

"aw"   thou̇ght⁵

"ow"   bou̇gh⁶

67

ti

"sh"   na tion

ti, si, ci say "sh" when they are
together for the sound. See page 4
in the notebook.

68

si

"sh"   ses sion

"zh"   vi sion²

ti, si, ci say "sh."
si is the only one which can say
"zh." See page 4 in the notebook.

69

ci

"sh"   fa cial

ti, si, ci say "sh." See page 4 in the
notebook.

CHAPTER IV

Handwriting

THE TEACHING of writing should precede reading. This is fundamental. It is the only approach to the printed or written language that is clear and understandable to all children. Writing brings into play the kinesthetic controls, that is, the use of the hand muscles, which are coordinated with those of the mouth when the child pronounces the sound of each phonogram before he writes it. Most children have some confusion in the proper sequence of letters in words for both reading and spelling, and this method overcomes such confusion. I follow a definite, detailed teaching pattern to prevent the numerous mistakes which otherwise are made so frequently that wrong habits are soon acquired.

I should like to say at this point that good and facile handwriting is a most important part of language. The lack of it is a constant handicap. It can be quickly acquired only if correct and exact techniques are well taught from the start, and well maintained at all times. The sounds of the phonograms are learned at the same time.

The Sounds and Formation of the Twenty-six Letters

Introduce handwriting by showing the class the printed twenty-six single-letter phonograms on the cards, saying all the sounds of each phonogram. Write each one in manuscript writing on the blackboard.

Before long you will do this while the children write it, just after they have repeated its sound. This familiarizes them with both the printed and written forms and their English sounds. No particular order or sequence is desirable after the first lesson.

Introduce all the lower case letters in the first lesson, if possible.

A few rules to guide a child in forming and placing the letters are a great help. The children are familiar with the clock face, and it is therefore useful in teaching how the letters are formed. Since the numbers on the clock are always in the same position, this makes an easy reference guide for children.

Many teachers fail to realize the importance of teaching the correct formation of the letters from the very start of teaching the written language. Unless children write correctly they do not *see* the correct symbols for the sounds. The best time to stop wrong habits is before they begin.

Bad motor patterns, once formed, are most difficult to correct later on. The teacher and children all gain from much patient supervision at this beginning stage.

The size and spacing of letters is important. For this reason the standard ruled paper where the lines are ⅜ths of an inch apart can be used from the beginning.

Every third line will be the base line for beginners in the first grade (or for beginners in handwriting at any grade), because at first children cannot easily form letters as small as those in normal adult writing. It is well for them to put a little pencil mark on the beginning of every third line of ruled paper so that they will know which lines to use as base lines. They should write the short letters to *fill* the space between the base line and the line above (⅜″ high), and the tall letters go to the second line above the base line.

Position for Both Left-handed and Right-handed Children

Sit with hips against the back of the chair. Put both feet on the floor but put no pressure on them, nor in the knees.

Sit with the head pushed up as high as possible so as to have *no* weight on the arms as they rest on the desk. Tip the body forward but keep it about two inches away from the desk.

Put both forearms on the desk, with elbows just off the front edge of the desk.

Keep the side of the paper parallel to the writing arm. (Like a railroad track, the arm is one track and the edge of the paper is the other.)

The left-handed child needs special attention. Be sure that he holds the side of his paper parallel to his writing arm. A strip of Scotch Tape pasted near the top of his desk to show the slanting direction to which the top edge of his paper should be parallel is a very useful aid to him. It keeps him from turning his paper like that of his right-handed neighbors. He should be watched to see that his writing hand is always below the base line on which he writes. He should also be told from the first that his letters can all be straight up and down or that he can use a slant provided the slant is backhand, and never forward. The forward slant, for a lefthanded writer, forces his hand into a most awkward, and hence wrong position.

The use of the hand which does not write is very important. It does the same work as a roller on a typewriter, i.e., it always *holds* the paper in position, and *moves it* back and forth and up and down on the desk so that the writing arm need never move up or down. The elbow of the writing arm like the hinge of the typewriter type bar (which puts the letter on the paper) has a fixed position.

The writing hand rests and slides on the ball of the palm and on the side of the little finger below the end joint. (This keeps the little finger from curling under too far and acting as a brake that prevents the hand from sliding easily across the paper. A mention of the way the brake on the bicycle stops the bicycle, helps the child feel what you are saying.)

How to Hold a Pencil

Hold the pencil between the thumb and the third finger. They are held opposite each other to form a vise. Round the index finger and avoid pinching the pencil. Hold it at the place where the paint

Correct writing position for left-handed child.

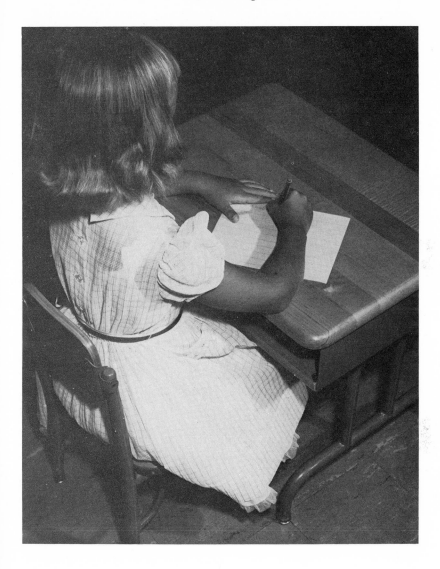

Correct writing position for right-handed child.

begins—about an inch from the point. The pencil should lie on the index finger just below the knuckle. This places the point of the pencil in the best position for writing. The sketches that follow are intended to illustrate this important matter to both teacher and pupil.

Keep the wrist flat (*not resting on the side!*) Make sure there is *no pressure* on the writing hand or arm. Teachers of little children ask them to make their arms and hands feel as light and soft as the leg and paw of a friendly kitten feels.

Position at the Blackboard

Stand about 18 inches away, no closer, and write at the eye level.

Curl fingers slightly. Lay the four fingers along the length of the chalk. The thumb is on the opposite side. This permits the use of the *side* of the point for writing.

All erasing should start at the top and move sideways in the direction in which we write. This applies also to erasing on paper. It prevents children looking at words backwards.

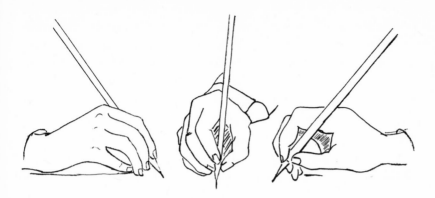

These sketches show how the pencil is held in the right hand.

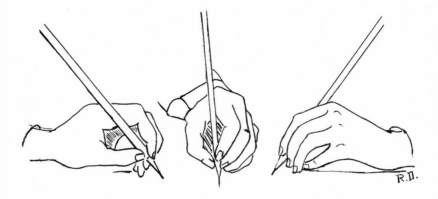

The pencil is held this way in the left hand.

Detailed Techniques of Teaching
the Lower-case Manuscript Letters

The teacher gives the general rules governing the letters.

All letters sit on the line.

Letters are of two sizes only. They are either *tall* or *short*. Tall letters reach two-thirds the way up to the base line above. Short letters are half as tall as tall letters. They occupy one-third of the space between the base lines. However beginners will at first make the letters three times larger, as stated before. This large size is used in the following directions.

Manuscript letters are made up of parts of the clock, and straight lines. The teacher's blackboard presentation should show this:

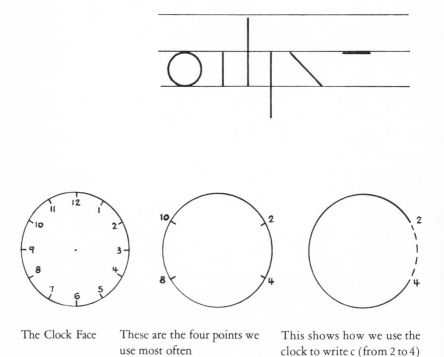

The Clock Face   These are the four points we use most often   This shows how we use the clock to write c (from 2 to 4)

Presentation of Letters that Begin at 2 on the Clock
Method: Teacher, holding up card a, says the three
sounds: "ă, ā, ah" (Say them in a staccato manner, not
run together).

Teacher: "I will show you how this letter is written. It is
a short letter. Short letters fill the space from the base line
to the line above. Start far enough in from the edge of
your paper to make a circle, which looks like the clock-
face. Start at 2, go up and all the way around the clock to
2 again; from there pull a line straight down to the base
line and leave it."
The class says the three sounds for a and each child writes
a on his paper.

Teacher then holds up card c and says the two sounds:
"k, s."
The class repeats the two sounds of c.
This is a short letter. Start just far enough from a to make
a clock. Begin at 2 and go up and around the clock and
stop at 4.

Teacher holds up card d and gives its sound, "d."
Help the children to see that the round part comes first.
Get each child to feel his tongue making a circle within
his mouth as he says "d." (b begins with a line and in
saying "b" the lips make a straight line. The kinesthetic
feel of these two letters can keep children from reversing
them. "d" begins with a circle and "b" begins with a
straight line.)
Start at 2 to make the short round part, go up and all the
way around the clock, go straight up to the second line
above, pull a line straight down to the base line, and
leave it.

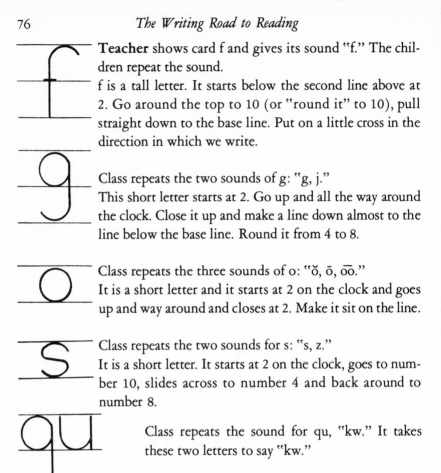

Teacher shows card f and gives its sound "f." The children repeat the sound.

f is a tall letter. It starts below the second line above at 2. Go around the top to 10 (or "round it" to 10), pull straight down to the base line. Put on a little cross in the direction in which we write.

Class repeats the two sounds of g: "g, j."
This short letter starts at 2. Go up and all the way around the clock. Close it up and make a line down almost to the line below the base line. Round it from 4 to 8.

Class repeats the three sounds of o: "ŏ, ō, ōō."
It is a short letter and it starts at 2 on the clock and goes up and way around and closes at 2. Make it sit on the line.

Class repeats the two sounds for s: "s, z."
It is a short letter. It starts at 2 on the clock, goes to number 10, slides across to number 4 and back around to number 8.

Class repeats the sound for qu, "kw." It takes these two letters to say "kw."

They are short letters. The first one starts at 2 on the clock, goes up and around and closes at 2. Without lifting the pencil make a straight line down to the line below and make a flag in the direction in which we write. The second letter sits close. Begin it with a down line, then round from 8 to 4, continue up with a straight line and finish on the base line with a straight down line.

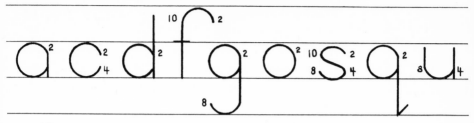

The teacher's explanation of how to use the numbers on the clock is indicated here.

The children's papers should look like this.

Teaching the Letters which Begin with Lines

Teach these line letters as soon as the "clock" letters have been presented well enough to establish in the child's mind the correct ways of forming them.

Letters which start with a line *sit close* to the preceding letter. All beginning lines start at the top. These are two important rules.

Do not take the pencil off the paper to complete any of these letters except in making the second part of k and to put the crosses on f, t and x.

Horizontal lines (including underlining, etc.) are always drawn in the direction of writing, (i.e., from left to right). Never use the words left or right. Instead establish "the direction in which we write", (and read), very firmly at the start. The beginning horizontal lines of e and z and the short crosses on t and f are drawn in the direction in which we write. Make certain that *no* child retraces these lines backwards because this reverses the habit he must acquire.

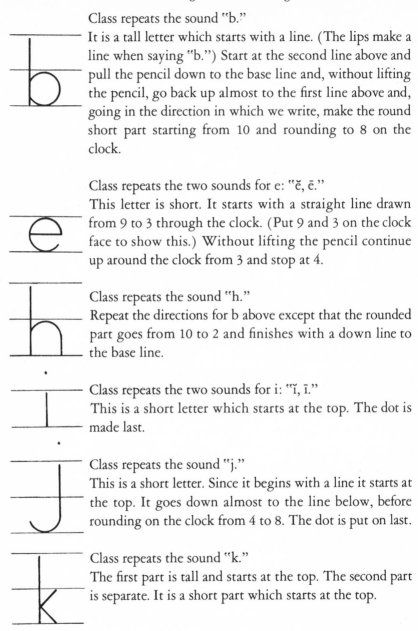

Class repeats the sound "b."

It is a tall letter which starts with a line. (The lips make a line when saying "b.") Start at the second line above and pull the pencil down to the base line and, without lifting the pencil, go back up almost to the first line above and, going in the direction in which we write, make the round short part starting from 10 and rounding to 8 on the clock.

Class repeats the two sounds for e: "ĕ, ē."

This letter is short. It starts with a straight line drawn from 9 to 3 through the clock. (Put 9 and 3 on the clock face to show this.) Without lifting the pencil continue up around the clock from 3 and stop at 4.

Class repeats the sound "h."

Repeat the directions for b above except that the rounded part goes from 10 to 2 and finishes with a down line to the base line.

Class repeats the two sounds for i: "ĭ, ī."

This is a short letter which starts at the top. The dot is made last.

Class repeats the sound "j."

This is a short letter. Since it begins with a line it starts at the top. It goes down almost to the line below, before rounding on the clock from 4 to 8. The dot is put on last.

Class repeats the sound "k."

The first part is tall and starts at the top. The second part is separate. It is a short part which starts at the top.

Class repeats the sound "l."

It is a tall line which starts at the top and sits on the base line.

Class repeats the sound "m."

It is a short letter that begins with a line. It starts at the top and is drawn straight down to the base line. Retrace to the top and round it on the clock from 10 to 2, continue by making a straight line to the base line, retrace to the top of the line, round again from 10 to 2 on the clock and finish with a straight line which ends at the base line.

Class repeats the sound "n."

This is a short letter. Repeat the directions for making the first part of m above.

Class repeats the sound "p." It is a short letter.

It starts with a line and therefore sits close to the preceding letter. The line starts at the top and goes to the line below the base line. Retrace on this line to the top and round the second part from 10 to 8 on the clock.

Class repeats the sound "r."

This is a short letter which starts at the top. Make the short line go to the base line, retrace to the top and round it from 10 to 2 on the clock.

Class repeats the sound "t."

This is a tall letter. It begins at the top. The cross is small and drawn in the direction in which we write.

Class repeats the three sounds for u: "ŭ, ū, ŏŏ."
This is a short letter. It starts with a line at the top. Bring the line almost to the base line and round it from 8 to 4, continue up with a straight line and retrace with a line to the base line.

Class repeats the sound for v.
This is a short letter. It starts with a line and therefore it is started at the top and sits close to the preceding letter. The first line slants in the direction in which we write. Finish without lifting the pencil.

Class repeats the sound of w. The teacher gives the same directions she gave for "v."

Class repeats the sound of x: "ks."
It also is short and the first line starts at the top; therefore it sits close to the last letter and slants in the direction in which we write. The cross is made separately and it starts at the top.

Class repeats the three sounds for y: "y, ĭ, ī."
This is a short letter. Start it at the top with a straight line, then round the bottom from 8 to 4, go up with a straight line and straight down almost to the line below the base line, before rounding from 4 to 8 on the clock. (As a consonant, y has one sound; as a vowel, it has two sounds.)

Class repeats the sound "z."
This is a short letter. It starts with a line. Therefore it sits close to the preceding letter and the top line is made in the direction in which we write. Without taking the pencil off the paper make a slanted line to the base line at the point under the beginning of the top line, and finish with a line drawn in the direction in which we write. The top and bottom lines should be parallel.

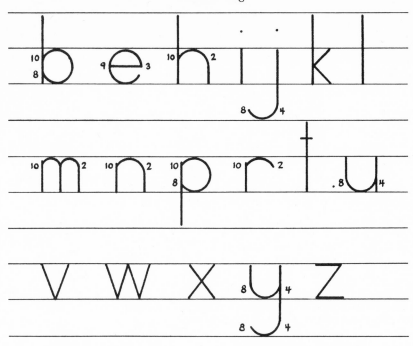

The teacher shows how the clock is used on the rounded parts.

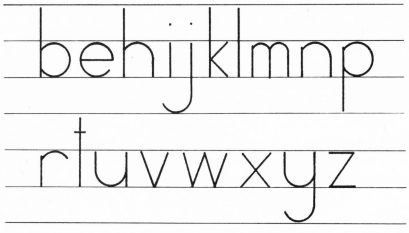

The children's papers should look like this.

I have gone into detail as to what to say to children who are learning to write because it is necessary to be specific if handwriting is to become a correct, facile tool for learning. If letters are made incorrectly, they are mentally pictured incorrectly also. This becomes one of the serious causes of failure in both reading and spelling—one of many reasons why correct writing is essential.

Those letters that begin at 2 on the clock have been shown and also those which begin with a line. Now write the alphabet across the page in order to teach the correct spacing of letters. The spacing of letters is taught from the first lesson. Letters that begin at 2 on the clock

start just far enough away from the preceding letter to form the clock. Letters that begin with a line sit very close to the preceding letter. Always say the sounds of the letters before writing them. (Note that q alone has no sound.)

The reader may wonder at the amount of detailed directions given to explain the teaching of writing. In these techniques and aids to writing will be found the simple direct system for helping any child acquire the correct motor patterns. Therefore it is worth while to include here every aid that has proven most valuable in teaching, even if the detail seems monotonous to an adult. The first and second grade and kindergarten teachers cannot afford to skip any of it. Handwriting is a basic means of overcoming the confusions and reversals in reading which so many children suffer from.

Techniques of Teaching the Manuscript Capital Letters

Be sure the lower-case letters are well learned before introducing all the capital letters.

It is necessary to teach some of the capital letters early, such as those needed for the first letters in writing a child's name.

When children learn that a capital is used only where the rules of English require it, they will not insert capitals indiscriminately. There is always a definite reason for using a capital letter. Children should be taught these reasons and be required to give the reason each time they use a capital.

All capital letters are tall. They fill the space between the base line and the second line above. (Shown below at half size.)

The rules for round lower case letters also apply to the following capital letters. They each start at 2 on the clock. (Give the sounds of each capital letter before writing it and have the children repeat these sounds before they write.) The cross on the Q starts at the top.

In writing capital letters beginning with lines make the vertical line first, starting at the top. The horizontal lines of A, E, F, H, I, T are made in the direction in which we write. Where there is more than one horizontal line, make the top one first. (E, F, I) The pencil is lifted before making the second lines of A, B, D, E, F, H, I, K, M, N, P, R, T, and they also begin at the top.

ABDEFHIJKL

MNPRTUy

The capital letters V, W and X are made just like their lower-case letters. First make the line which slants in the direction in which we write, starting at the top. V and W are made without lifting the pencil. The second line of X starts at the top.

Y is the only capital which is finished below the base line.

Z is formed the same as its lower-case letter. The top line is drawn in the direction in which we write and it is finished without taking the pencil off the paper.

Techniques of Teaching Numbers

Numbers should be as high as the tall letters. All numbers are the same height.

The numbers 8, 9 and 0 begin at 2 on the clock.

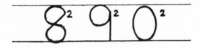

The rule for the spacing of numbers which begin at 2 on the clock is the same as for manuscript letters. Start just far enough away to make a clock.

The numbers 1, 4, 5 and 6 begin with a line and all lines start at the top. The left-hand vertical line of 4 and 5 is drawn first. The horizontal line of the 5 is short and is drawn last and in the direction of writing.

The bottom of a 6 can end on the base line. Then it never looks like 0. 7 begins with a line drawn in the direction of writing.

The numbers which begin with a line sit very close to the preceding number. This is also true for 2 and 3.

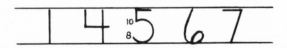

Numbers 2 and 3 begin at 10 on the clock. Note that no lowercase letter starts at 10 so these two numbers should be thoroughly understood by children who show confusion in direction.

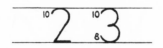

Now write all the numbers on a line showing the proper spacing. All except the last three which begin at 2 on the clock, start close to the preceding number.

1234567890

Before the children write 2 and 3 ask where these two numbers start until every child knows they begin at 10 on the clock. (Children who reverse these numbers can come to dislike arithmetic. It is very important to prevent this reversing.)

In itemizing or numbering pages, I do not put periods after whole numbers. In mathematics a period is a decimal point and it is read "and." 5.2 is read "five and two-tenths."

In writing the brain directs the hand. This cannot be done correctly unless there is a thorough knowledge of how each letter and number is made.

The child who has no difficulty in learning to write needs to be taught at first, but need not be held for drill. The children who need help should be given the specific directions in this chapter over and over until they can direct their hand in writing and no longer make errors in direction or orientation. This is where drill is an essential part of teaching, if children are to learn. The teacher has done no teaching unless and until the pupil learns.

After the first presentation, it is well to have small groups, in turn, write at the blackboard. Errors in writing can thus be readily caught and corrected.

After teaching the sounds and the writing of single manuscript letters the teacher presents all the other phonograms on the Seventy Cards in varying sequences, but in the same manner as the single letters were presented. The phonograms now should be written in two columns down the page rather than across the page. Have the children fold their papers down the middle and use the crease to line up the second column. The phonograms must be thoroughly learned with the accurate sounds and they must be correctly written (not copied).

Spacing has already been shown so that when a card of more than one letter is written the question "Where does the second or subsequent letter start?" should bring the response, "At 2 on the clock. Start just far enough out to make a clock" or "It begins with a line which sits close to the last letter. A line starts at the top."

When words are introduced the spacing of letters within a word follows the above rules. A space the size of one letter is left between words. (Show the children that on the typewriter, pressing the space bar once leaves such a space.) Children's papers are more easily read if they leave the space of two letters between sentences.

After children can easily form the letters correctly they should learn to reduce the size of their handwriting to one third the size of the above lower case letters. This reduced size is used in showing the cursive writing which follows.

Cursive Writing

Cursive writing follows the same rules for position as those given for manuscript writing.

The letters of connected (i.e., cursive) writing should be taught only after manuscript writing with the phonogram sounds has been perfected by long practice and no longer requires any special attention. This can usually be after Christmas in the second grade. Children want to learn cursive writing. A promise to teach it as soon as they perfect the basic manuscript writing is an incentive to a real effort to improve.

All the letters within a word in cursive alphabet writing are connected together.

The connecting lines from the end of one letter to the right place to start the next letter are of five kinds:

a short upswing from the base line,

a tall upswing from the base line,

a short upswing which curves on over to 2 on the clock,

a short dip kept at the height of a short letter across to the start of the next letter, or as an ending on the letters: b, o, v and w.

the short dip that curves on over to 2 on the clock.

All vertical lines start at the top and are drawn straight down to the base line before starting the sharp curve up.

All letters which go below the base line and curve back up, cross at the underside of the base line at the point where the down line has crossed the base line.

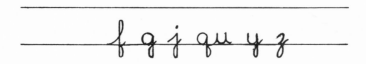

The vertical lines in cursive writing can be slanted forward for the right-handed child. All such lines are parallel to each other. Left-handed writers can write straight up and down. If they develop a slant it must be back hand, never forward.

Most of the differences between manuscript and cursive writing are shown by the dotted lines in the cursive letters below. The solid lines show to what extent the letters are alike.

abcdefghijklmnopqrstuvwxyz

abcdefghijklmnopqrstuvwxyz

Cursive writing is easily taught by having the children write the entire manuscript alphabet and then write over it the cursive letters with connecting lines and other changes, as shown above. The differences are readily seen. Be sure all the sounds of each letter are spoken just before it is written.

acdghijlmnopqutuvwxy

befkrsz

The forms of a, c, d, g, h, i, j, l, m, n, o, p, qu, t, u, v, w, x, y are essentially the same in cursive writing and in manuscript. The letters b, e, f, k, r, s and z are changed the most, and need more attention.

v and w are written the same as in manuscript except that the lower sharp points are rounded and they end with a dip at the top.

b, e, f, h, k and l start with an upswing which makes a sharp curve backward at the top to start the straight down line.

g, j, y and z are the letters which end with a straight line down below the base line and take a sharp curve backward at the bottom and up to connect to the next letter. This up curve crosses the down line exactly at the base line.

f and q turn forward and swing up, meeting the down line exactly at the base line. The q turns at the bottom as did the flag in the manuscript form.

d and p have no loops.

a, c, d, g, o, and q, letters which in manuscript begin at 2 on the clock, also can begin at 2 in cursive writing when they are the first letters of words.

m, n, u, v, w, x and y may also be made without an initial up line from the base line at the beginning of a word.

m, n and x start with a slight curve.

All down lines are straight lines. If they are slanted the slant should be the same for each down line.

All letters at the end of a word or when written alone end with a small upswing from the base line except b, o, v, w, which end with a dip kept at the height of a short letter.

Spacing between words can and should be closer in cursive than in manuscript writing because the end of a word is shown by the absence of a connecting line to the first letter of the next word.

Teachers obtain the attention and effort of their children through their personality and interesting ways of teaching. Teaching requires a little dramatizing to open children's minds for learning. A good teacher intuitively senses whether what she is saying is listened to, is understood, and is likely to be retained. This seems especially true in teaching these language arts.

When we let children write and read they are learning to use the tools by which they will acquire an education. We never call anything we do in this regard a game. We want to start to develop disciplined minds.

The Capital Letters in Cursive Writing

A²n Bi Co² D E²m F Ge

Hi In Jo Ki L²a Mo² No

O² P ²Qu Ro² Si Th Un

V W X Ye ²Za

Certain capital letters in cursive writing do not connect to the next letter. These are D, F, O, P, V and W.

The capital letters D, E, F, T, G, I, J, L and Q are different forms from the small letters or manuscript letters.

D starts with a straight down line and is completed without lifting the pencil.

E and L begin at 2 on the clock.

I and J are the only letters that begin at the base line with a backward upswing and curve forward at the top. (All upswings for lower-case cursive letters are forward.) I and J should be carefully taught together. As lower-case letters they are the only ones which are dotted. As capitals they are the only ones that begin with a backward upswing.

G and S start alike with an upswing from the base line.

T and F begin with a dip at the top.

Q and Z begin at 10 on the clock as do the numbers 2 and 3.

Other Writing Hints

A comma is a tiny half-clock. It starts on the line comfortably close to the letter it follows, and goes below the line rounding from 12 to 6 on the clock.

When the children first write a period, say, "A period is made by setting the pencil on the line comfortably close to the letter it follows, and taking the pencil up." This keeps children from setting commas and periods just any place, and also gives a precise kinesthetic feel to them. It also helps them to see commas and periods on the printed page.

I am convinced that teachers must demonstrate and explain much more about how each letter, number and punctuation mark should be formed and placed. The strange, awkward ways in which nearly all children contrive to form some of their letters shows their need of all these techniques of handwriting.

The first letter written on a page should be written carefully because every letter that follows should be of the same relative size.

Every round letter should fit on the same-sized clock.

Tall letters and capitals are twice as high as short letters.

All letters which go below the base line go just as far below the base line as short letters go above it.

I have given a great deal of study to the techniques of teaching good and easy handwriting, not only for its own sake but also for the facility for self-expression and for clarifying of one's ideas that come from a command of easy, readable writing. The prime reason is that it is the simplest direct means of learning the sounds of English as they are represented in our written language. I do not know of another book on handwriting which at every point ties in the sounds of the letters with their form. And yet what meaning can the form of a letter have unless it conveys its sound to the child as he learns to write it? This is one of the reasons why writing is the logical road to reading.

CHAPTER V

Spelling and the Child's Notebook

THIS CHAPTER demonstrates in detail the method by which each child above the second grade writes the first seven pages in his own notebook every year. It is his own reference book for the phonograms and for the rules of spelling and pronunciation. (The teachers in the first two grades put appropriate parts of these pages on the blackboard and then on charts for ready reference in teaching the rules of spelling as they are needed.)

Spelling rules, explanatory notes and instructions for the teacher are given along with each page of the model of the child's first seven pages of his notebook.

The teachers in the first and second grades, as well as those in the upper grades, need to be fully conversant with this entire notebook and its explanations in order to teach and explain correctly any word that comes up in speech, writing or reading.

It should be noted here that pages 1, 2, 5, 6 and 7 of the notebook are basic. Their contents are taught from the start in all grades even though the children in the first two grades do not write this part in a notebook.

I want to emphasize that the teacher or parent who gives careful attention to the procedure and meticulously follows all the major and

94

minor details of teaching for the mental and physical production of this notebook, will be well rewarded. Progress of each and all of her pupils will henceforth make her work much lighter and a source of pleasure. The mastery of the notebook is the key to the child's success in his use of the language arts. This is where competent teaching really counts.

In presenting the writing of the notebook to the children of the third grade and each higher grade, the teacher should tell what the purpose of the notebook is. (I have taught many classes of high-school students and many young people of college age who have needed and have written this notebook.) It is presented in manuscript unless the students already know cursive writing.

I teach manuscript writing at first to each student no matter what his age. The older student needs manuscript for lettering maps, diagrams and drawings, but chiefly it makes a needed visible link between his writing and all printed matter. All children should first write the phonograms given on the cards in manuscript. This gives them a kinesthetic connection between the sounds and printed forms for reading. For those with any reading handicap this is highly important.

Detailed Technique for Teaching Page One

The first page lists the single consonants at the top. It gives the single vowels and words to show the important sounds of each vowel. At the bottom of the page are listed the five kinds of silent final e's.

The teacher tells the children that the first word "Consonants" is the title or name for the next line of letters. The word Consonants goes in the middle of the top line. Since it is a title, we write it with a capital. We divide it into syllables.

A syllable is that part of a word or a single word which is capable of being pronounced by a single impulse of the voice. Once when teaching a group of ninth-grade boys who had no idea what a syllable was I used my hands to indicate the beat of the syllables. Take the word consonants. After the class says, "con" the teacher, facing the class, makes a down beat with her right hand. The class says "so" and her left hand makes a down beat. For "nants" she crosses the right over the left for the final beat. The children, in showing syllables in this manner, start with the left hand, then the right and then the left crossed over the right hand. This kinesthetic effect has proven helpful to many children and can even be used with pre-school children to establish correct pronunciation.

To go a step further in the kinesthetic feel of a word the teacher holds up three fingers of her right hand showing that it takes three letters to write the first syllable and points to the finger on her right. The children say the sound "c"; as she points to the next finger they say "ŏ"; and as she points to the next one they say the sound "n." Then the teacher holds up two fingers of her left hand. She points to the one to her right and the children say the sound "s." She then points to the other finger and the children say "ō" showing there are two letters to write so. Then crossing the right hand over the left she holds up five fingers for nants and points to each in turn as the children give the individual sounds.

These procedures give children who have difficulty learning to spell a chance to think what the writing must be, before they actually write. Such reasoning keeps children from making errors which once made must be supplanted later. This is good teaching.

The teacher asks the children to give her the first syllable of Consonants. When she gets the reply "Con," she writes it on the board. At the same time the children are writing it in their notebooks. (They write while she is writing because they are not to copy her writing.) While writing Con, the teacher asks for the second syllable. When she gets the reply "so," she puts it on the board while the children write it in their books. While writing so, the teacher asks for the third syllable. When she gets the reply "nants," they write nants while she writes it, and they sound out "n," "ă," "n," "t," "s." This helps them to write it accurately. This sounding of the phonograms should always be done with any syllable which presents a difficulty in accurate pronunciation or in writing.

The teacher then says, "On the next line we will write the single consonants." (These are printed in order on the first 21 phonogram cards.) She asks, "The first consonant in the alphabet says what?" as she holds up the card b. The children give the sound "b" (not "bŭ") and write the letter. She then shows the card c and the children say "k", "s" for the two sounds of c and write the letter c. (Since no consonant ever uses its name for its sound, we never say the names of these letters when it is possible to use their sounds instead.)

The children should know the phonograms and give the sounds in unison. Before they write, they are reminded of how each letter is made in case any child is not sure of it. Continue writing the rest of the consonants in the same manner.

On the third and fourth lines write, "c before e, i or y says $\overset{2}{c}$. If g is before e, i or y it may say $\overset{2}{g}$." The teacher has the children say and write each of the phonograms in these words as they are written. She will have previously studied the Ayres list (which follows in Chapter VI) and will know how to teach these words just as described in Chapter VI. The above description of writing the word "Consonants" is identical with this, except that in one-syllable words each phonogram is sounded before it is written.

The teacher tells what is to be written and where. Everything which is written must also serve as continued training in the accurate writing of the sounds and sequences of speech.

On the next line the children write the title "Vowels" using exactly the same procedure as described for the title "Consonants." Here we put a 2 above the s. In this case and where figures above phonograms may be written hereafter, the figure above a phonogram indicates that the word uses the phonogram's second sound or the third, etc. These sounds are always numbered in the sequence as listed on the backs of the phonogram cards. When no figure is written above, it signifies that the first sound is the one used in the word. (Numbers are not needed above the phonograms c and g because simple rules tell which sound to use.)

The single vowels are on the phonogram cards 20, and 22 to 27.

The five kinds of silent final e have a special way of being numbered. On all seven pages of the notebook and also in the Ayres list in Chapter VI, all these silent final e's are identified by the numbers 2, 3, 4 or 5 written below them. If the e belongs to the first kind of silent e, no number is put under it.

The other pages of the Child's Notebook are presented in the same manner as described above.

Notes to Teachers about Page One

This page presents the twenty-one single-letter consonants, the six single-letter vowels, and the five kinds of silent final e's.

This is a spelling notebook. In it words when written alone are divided into syllables so that the relationship between the sounds and the symbols can be readily seen.

Each consonant has but a single sound except c, g and s. The Rules 2 and 3 below make it unnecessary to number the second sounds of c and g. Only s when it says "z" needs a 2 placed above it when learning to pronounce and write words.

I avoid using the terms "name" of a letter, "the long vowel" or "short vowel." Instead I use the sound itself because the other words are only names for sounds and are thus less direct.

The children must learn and understand and always apply the following seven rules.

Rule 1. q is always written with two letters qu when we say the sound "kw." The u is not considered a vowel here.

Rule 2. When c by itself has a sound, it always says "s" if followed by e, i or y (cent, city, cyclone); otherwise its sound is "k" (cat, cyclone, music).

A model of Page One of the
Child's Notebook.

Con so nants

b c d f g h j k l m n p qu r s t v w x y z
c before e, i or y says ĉ, and
if g is before e, i or y it may say g̊

Vow els̊

a	at	na vy	wånt
e	end	me	
i	{ In di an	si lent	
y	{ ba by	my	
o	odd	o pen	dŏ
u	up	mu s̊ic	půt

Silent final e {
time
have
blue
chance
charge
lit tle
are (no job e)

In many words ci is pronounced "sh", and then it is a two-letter phonogram and thus does not have either sound of c. ch is always a two-letter phonogram. Rule 2 applies only where c is a single phonogram.

Rule 3. When g has a sound by itself it can say "j" only if it is followed by e, i or y. When followed by any other letter, it says "g." (Get, girl and give prove that there are a few exceptions to this rule.) In spelling if g is used to say "j," it must be followed by e, i or y, as in pigeon, religious.

These rules 2 and 3 are most valuable. They enable the child to know the correct sound for c and g by means of the letter that follows. The teacher should ask for these rules until the children apply them automatically, in both writing and reading.

The vowels are underlined in key words only when they say their name at the end of a syllable. The child learns the sounds of the vowels in the order given. The first one is used most frequently. A child may need to say the key word to prove that his sound is accurate until he is sure of each sound. For example if he does not say the ŭ in just correctly he can help himself by saying the first sound of the key word, up and then sounding "j" "ŭ" "s" "t."

Rule 4. Vowels a, e, o, u usually say "ā," "ē," "ō," "ū" at the end of a syllable. The second key word shows this: (na̱ vy, me̱, o̱ pen, mu̱ sic.) This is one of the three ways a vowel may say ā, ē, ī, ō or ū.

Rule 5. i and y can say "ī" at the end of the syllable but usually they say "ĭ." This is shown at the end of the second syllable of both Indĭan and babў.

Rule 6. y, not i, is used at the end of an English word.

Rule 7. There are five kinds of silent e. In short words, as me, she, he, the e says "ē" but in all longer words where a single e appears at the end, the e is silent. (There are very few exceptions.) In Chaucer's day they were sounded. Now they are silent. As shown below we retain the first four kinds of silent e's because we need them. The fifth kind is probably a relic from Chaucerian days.

1) time. This is an "ī," then a consonant, and a final e. The silent e is put there to make the i say "ī" instead of ĭ. This is true in late, here, style, rose, tune. The single vowels before any single consonant can say "ā," "ē," "ī," "ō" or "ū" if a silent e follows to end the base word. (Sometimes there are two consonants between as in paste or bathe. These words are past and bath when the silent e is omitted.)

2) have, blue. In English we cannot end a word with v or the single vowel u. We add a silent e. (Impromptu is one of the few exceptions.)

3) chance, charge. The silent e follows c and g to make them say "s" and "j." Without the e, the last sounds would be "k" and "g." Rules 2 and 3 show this. At the end of a base word we could use only e as a silent letter. (i cannot sit at the end of a word and y always has a sound at the end of a word.)

4) lit tle. Every syllable in English must contain at least one vowel. ble, cle, dle, fle, gle, kle, ple, sle, tle and zle are the only syllables where neither of the first two letters is a vowel and the silent e is added in each so they can be separate syllables.

5) are. The e is not needed for any of the above reasons. It has no job and we call it the "no job e." House, come, promise are other examples of silent e's which perform no useful purpose in present-day English.

All of the above facts about our language can be learned from page one. The teacher should make constant reference to this page and to the six pages that follow to illustrate facts about our language as the children learn to write and read. This gives them understanding and security in speaking, writing and reading.

A model of Page Two of the
Child's Notebook.

Her	first	nurse₅
fern	third	hurt
herd	bird	burn
din ner	girl	church
berth	birth	turn
west ern	fir	fur
merge₃	thirst	pur pose₅
perch	firm	hur dle₄
gro cer y	squirm	sur prise
serv ice₃	squirt	Thurs day
verse₅	chirp	Sat ur day
nerve₂	cir cle₄	fur ther
nerv ous	sir	oc cur
ster ling	con firm	fur nish
per fect	skirt	dis turb
clerk		sub urb
cer tain		cur tain

works	early.
worm	learn
word	heard
world	search
worth	earn
wor thy	ear nest
worse	pearl
worst	earth
wor ry	re hears al
wor ship	

Notes to the Teacher about Page Two

Her first nurse works early.

This sentence gives five spellings of the sound "er" and it should be memorized. Their phonogram cards are numbered 27 to 32. The spelling er is used most often.

Rule 8. or may say "er" when w comes before the or, as in works. There are few other guides in the choice of the spelling of the sound "er."

First dictate the sentence containing the five spellings of the sound "er." It sits on the top line of this page. Teach each word as described for teaching words on page one. Then dictate the five words across the second line, and so on.

Check the children's knowledge of this page by asking, for example, "Which "er" is in church?" The answer is, "The one in nurse." (The word in the model sentence at the top of the page.) Do this same checking with any word having an "er" sound.

For children who find spelling difficult it is advisable to consider or and ar as having only the sounds as in for and far—not the sound er as in doctor and collar. In speaking, the or of doctor and the ar of collar deteriorate in sound because the accent is on the first syllable. In writing them say "doc tor" and "col lar."

Notes to the Teacher about Page Three

First dictate the four headings of the columns, then the top word of each of the first three columns, then the three words on the line below and so on for the three columns. Then dictate the exceptions from top to bottom. Children readily learn the nonsensical sentence given and learn that all these words plus the few at the bottom of the column contain ei. From the headings on this page it can be seen that there are three places for the use of the phonogram ei. The cards 56 and 57 show the three sounds each for ie and ei and two of these are the same for both phonograms. Therefore the sound alone cannot show which of these spellings to use. Rule 9 helps to decide which phonogram to use.

Rule 9. After c we use ei. If we say "ā" we can use ei, but never ie. In the list of exceptions we use ei. In all other words we use ie.

---

ie is "ĕ" in fri̱end. Put two lines under it. These double lines are used to mark any such phonogram which has an uncommon sound that is not given on the phonogram cards.

eigh is not considered on this page because this phonogram should say "ā." It is not ei alone. In foreign the ei has a sound, and the gn has a sound. They are not one sound as is eigh.

The teacher will test each child by asking which spelling, ie or ei, is used in the listed words. Example: Which is used in receive? In answering the child should say, ei because it comes after c; or, if the word is brief, he will say "ie because it comes after r and not after c, also the sound is not "ā," and it is not one of the exceptions."

I find that if children, in this way, apply and state these rules often enough they will begin to apply them when they write. It is the old problem of teaching children to think before they write or speak. It helps them develop the vital habit of using their minds in what they do and say.

I have asked many children in classes and individually how they know when to use ie or ei. Almost all know the rhyme ī before ē except after c, or when sounded as ā, etc. Then I have asked, "Which do you use after c?" It was a year and a half after I began asking this in the six upper grades in several schools before any child was able to give me the answer. So you see a rule that is not understood and used is of small value.

A model of Page Three of the
Child's Notebook.

We use ei after c,— — — —

ie	cei
be lieve	re ceive
be lief	per ceive
fierce	ceil ing
brief	re ceipt
niece	con ceit
priest	
field	
siege	
friend	
chief	
a chieve	
piece	
pie	
lie	
prai rie	

_ _ _ _ _ if the sound is "ā," _ _ _ _ _ _ _ _ and in some exceptions.

ei says "ā"	Exceptions	
their (they)	Nei ther	
veil	for eign	
skein	sov er eign	Learn
heir (in her it)	seized	this
{ rein	(the) coun ter feit	as a
{ reign	(and) for feit ed	sentence
vein	lei sure.	
sur veil lance		
	ei ther	
	weird	
	heif er	

Notes for the Teacher about Page Four

This page explains the usual spellings for the sound "sh" at the beginning of any syllable after the first one. Cards No. 67, 68 and 69 show these.

Dictate these words, after the column headings and a general discussion of Rules 10 through 13, by going from top to bottom of each column in turn. (Be sure the words are dictated as said in conversation, but that the children say each separate syllable just before they write it.)

Rule 10. sh is used at the beginning of a base word and at the end of a syllable (she, finish) but, except in the ending ship (friendship, worship,) it is not used at the beginning of any syllable after the first.

Rule 11. ti, si and ci are the phonograms most frequently used to say "sh" at the beginning of a second or subsequent syllable.

Rule 12. si is used to say "sh" when the syllable before it ends in s (ses si̱on) and when the base word has an s at the point where the base word i̱s changed (tense, ten si̱on).

Rule 13. si̱ saying "zh" is on this page to remind us that si is the only common phonogram for the "zh" sound (di vi si̱on).

---

ci is used in gracious and facial because the base words, grace and face, have c where the change comes.

In some words no rule governs the choice of ti, si, or ci for the sound "sh" and the spelling must be memorized, as in influential.

It is important that the vowel sound in each of the last syllables of the words on this page be said accurately.

Vĕ ne ti̱an (ă), im pa ti̱ent (ĕ), gra ci̱o̱us (ŭ)

The first s of conscious and conscientious is silent. The ci of associate and of conscientious say "sh" but since there is no vowel except the i of ci in these syllables, the i is sounded. The syllable ci says "shĭ."

Is the cie in the word ancient an exception to Rule 9 illustrated on page 3 in the notebook? No, because this is ci followed by an e which fact we know from their sounds in this syllable. Unless the phonograms are sounded aloud many rules of spelling do not make sense. It is the failure to combine the sounds with the spelling of English which makes it seem so difficult to learn and makes so many common words seem to be exceptions to the general rules of spelling. This is another good reason why it is important always to teach any new word by writing its spoken sounds.

The use of the sounds of the phonograms permits the child to see clearly the relationship between the spoken word, the writing of the word and the reading of it.

After every lesson in the making and using of the notebook, each listed word written should be read aloud by the child, first in syllables and then again as the word is said in conversation. He should also use the word in a sentence which shows that he knows its meaning.

A model of Page Four of the
Child's Notebook.

sh is used at the beginning of a base word,
at the end of a syllable but not at the begin
of any syllable after the first one. ti, si and

ti	si
na tion	ses sion
im par tial	com pres sion
sub stan tial	dis cus sion
pa la tial	de pres sion
po ten tial	ad mis sion
pa tience $=_3$	
tor ren tial	ten sion (tense) $=_5$
in fec tious	tran sient (trans it)
in flu en tial	man sion (manse) $=_5$
am bi tion	
su per sti tious	
con fi den tial	$\overset{2}{s}i$
col lec tion	
Ve ne tian	di vi $\overset{2}{s}$ion
	oc ca $\overset{2}{s}$ion
	ex plo $\overset{2}{s}$ion

usually used to say "sh" at the beginning of a syllable after the first one.

---

ci

ăn cient

ra cial

so cial

fi nan cial

{ gla cial

{ gla cier

e lec tri cian   ce

fa cial

gra cious   o cean

phy si cian

mu si cian

pro fi cien cy

con scious

as so ci ate

con sci en tious

Notes to the Teacher about Page Five

This page shows when final consonants are doubled when certain endings are added to base words.

Rule 14. Words of one syllable (like hop), ending in one consonant, which have only one vowel before this last consonant, double the last consonant before adding an ending that begins with a vowel.

The order of dictating the words on Page 5 is important. The base words on the left-hand page are dictated first. Then dictate the endings which begin with a vowel and discuss how we add the appropriate endings to the base words. (Reasoning is required to use Rules 14, 15 and 16).

Now dictate the second column on the left-hand page. The children should understand that they are using Rule 14 as they write. A quite different intellectual process is required in writing the double consonant in base words, such as the two l's of village or trolley.

The child must learn that he doubles the p in "hopping" to preserve the vowel sound of the base word hop (ŏ). If the p is not doubled the word is hopē̱d whose base word is hope as shown on Page 6.

Writ is the archaic past tense of write. We still use "writ" as a noun. Explaining this can help to show why we say "writ ten."

Check to see that the child understands Rule 14. Ask, "How do you add the ending ment to ship?" The child's answer should be, "We do not double the p of ship because ment is not one of the endings which requires it. ment begins with a consonant, not a vowel."

Ask, "How do we add "ĕd" to talk?" The child should reply, "We do not double the k since this base word ends in two consonants, not just one."

Ask, "How do we add "er" to red?" The child replies, "We double the "d" since red has one syllable, one consonant at the end, one vowel before the last consonant and the ending begins with a vowel. Rule 14 can be called the one, one, one rule.

Rule 15. Words of two syllables, like "begin," where the second syllable gin is like hop, having one consonant at the end and one vowel before it, also double this last consonant before adding an ending that begins with a vowel, if the accent is on the last syllable.

Americans use this rule more consistently than do the English.

Ask the children to clap the rhythm of two-syllable words where the above rule applies as they pronounce them. (Notice that acquit conforms to the rule since the qu is a consonant sound. The u is not considered a vowel here.)

Words that have the accent on the first syllable, but otherwise would fit the rule, should be clapped also. We should not double the consonant in these words when adding an ending beginning with a vowel:

en' ter, prof' it, can' cel, trav' el

A model of Page Five of the
Child's Notebook.

Words of one syllable, ending in one conso[r]
which have only one vowel before this last
sonant (like hop), double the last consonan[t]
fore adding an ending that begins with a v[o]

hop	hop ping	hopped
run	run ning	
stop	stopped	stop page
red	red dish	
hot	hot test	
mud	mud dy	
flat	flat ten	
drug	drug gist	
ship	shipped	ship per
writ	writ ten	

Endings which begin with a vowel	ing	ice	ous
	er	ish	ist
	3)ed	age	i ble
	est	ance	a ble
	y	ant	a bly
	al	ence	an cy
	en	ent	en cy

Words of two syllables, (like begin, where the second syllable gin is like hop, having one consonant at the end and one vowel before it), also double this last consonant before adding an ending which begins with a vowel, if the accent is on the last syllable.

be gin'	be gin ning
ad mit'	ad mit tance
ac quit'	ac quit tal
oc cur'	oc cur rence
ex cel'	ex cel lent
trans mit'	trans mit ter
for got'	for got ten
con trol'	con trol la ble
re mit'	re mit ted

Notes to the Teacher about Page Six

Rule 16. Words ending with one of the five kinds of silent e's drop the e when adding an ending that begins with a vowel. (hope—hoping)

The child must be well taught to see that these endings are appended to a base word, and to recognize what that base word is.

Sometimes we cannot drop the e. Changeable holds the e to let the g say "j," since able begins with a vowel, but not an e, i, or y which would permit g to say "j." (See Rule 3) Such exceptions can be easily understood by children who know the basic rules about c and g.

The e of hope is dropped for the past tense ending "ĕd." In hopĕd the e has two functions. It permits the o to say "ō" as well as forming "ĕd" as an ending.

The dictionary says to drop the final e of fierce to add the ending est, but in speaking, to put the c on the last syllable. This allows us (under Rule 2) to keep the "s" sound of c instead of its k sound.

Rules 14, 15 and 16 should be taught and well understood as they are needed even in the first grade. Pages 5 and 6 along with Pages 1 and 2 of the Notebook are basic for all grades.

A parent or teacher who is under the impression that six-year-olds lack the mental ability to learn, understand and apply such rules will be surprised and delighted to see how quickly they all do so, and how keen they are about demonstrating this ability to use reasoning in their work.

ords like hope which end with a silent e, drop
e e when an ending beginning with a vowel is
ded.

A model of Page Six of the
Child's Notebook.

hope	hoped hop ing
sire	de sired de sir ing
erve	nerv ous
have	be hav ior
erce	fierc er fierc est
ase	eas y
ome	com ing
nange	chang ing
erve	serv ice
hearse	re hears al
t tle	set tling set tler
ite	writ ing

Endings beginning with a vowel	{	ing ice ous
		er ish ist
		3)ed age i ble
		est {ance {a ble
		y {ant {a bly
		al {ence {an cy
		en {ent {en cy

118

A model of Page Seven of the
Child's Notebook.

Additional Common Phonograms. The number preceding a phonogram tells how many sounds it has.

sh	3) oo
ee	
2) th	3) ch
{ ay / ai	ng
	3) ea
2 { ow / 4 ou	ar
	ck
{ oy / oi	3) ed
{ aw / au	or
	wh
2 { ew / 2 ui	oa

3) ey   { ti
3) ei   2) si
3) ie   ci

  igh
  eigh

{ kn   6) ough
{ gn

  wr

  ph
                              { eu
  dge   For   pn
        Grade VI {   rh
  oe   and above qu^2
  gh x^2

Notes to the Teacher about Page Seven

The single consonants are listed on page one of the Child's Notebook and words containing these sounds are on the phonogram cards. The single vowels (with words to prove their sounds) are also on page one of the Child's Notebook.

Page two of the Child's Notebook gives five spellings of the sound "er" and a sentence showing all five, which the children learned, (Her first nurse works early.)

The phonograms on this page are all those not given on the first and second pages. They are numbered 32 through 70 on the phonogram cards. All the 70 phonograms are now in the Notebook and thus readily available at all times for both teacher and children.

The following examples of the sounds of these phonograms in words are for the teacher. The words should not be taught to the child because he should not associate these phonograms with any special word. He is to know them, and their sounds, when he writes or sees them in any word.

sh	(di<u>sh</u>)
ee	(s<u>ee</u>)
th	(<u>th</u>in, <u>th</u>is) ²
ay	(d<u>ay</u>) used at the end of a syllable.
ai	(p<u>ai</u>nt) Used in the middle of a word, never at the end.
ow	(n<u>ow</u>², l<u>ow</u> "ō")
ou	(r<u>ou</u>nd "ow"², f<u>ou</u>r "ō,"³ y<u>ou</u> "ōō," c<u>ou</u>n try "ŭ"⁴)
oy	(b<u>oy</u>) Used at the end of a syllable.
oi	(p<u>oi</u>nt) Used in the middle of a syllable.
aw	(l<u>aw</u>)
au	(f<u>au</u>lt)

ew   (gre̲w̲ "o͞o," ne̲w̲[2] "ū")
ui   (fru̲it "o͞o," su̲it[2] "ū")

oo   (bo̲o̲t "o͞o," fo̲o̲t[2] "o͞o," flo̲o̲r[3] "ō")
ch   (muc̲h̲, sc̲h̲ool[2] "k," c̲h̲iv al ry[3] "sh")

ng   (ra̲n̲g̲)
ea   (e̲a̲st "ē," he̲a̲d[2] "ĕ," bre̲a̲k[3] "ā")
ar   (fa̲r̲)
ck   (nec̲k̲ "k") Used only after a single vowel when it does not say its name.

ed   (grad e̲d̲, love̲d̲[2] "d," wrecke̲d̲[3] "t")

or   (o̲r̲)
wh   (w̲h̲en)

oa   (bo̲a̲t "ō")

ey   (the̲y̲ "ā," ke̲y̲[2] "ē," val le̲y̲[3] "ĭ")

ei   (con ce̲i̲t "ē," ve̲i̲l[2] "ā," for fe̲i̲t[3] "ĭ")
ie   (fi̲e̲ld "ē," pi̲e̲[2] "ī," lil i̲e̲s[3] "ĭ")

igh   (si̲g̲h̲ "ī"
eigh   (we̲i̲g̲h̲ "ā")

kn   (k̲n̲ot "n") Used only at the beginning of a base word.
gn   (g̲n̲at "n")

wr   (w̲r̲ite "r")

ph   (p̲h̲an tom "f")

dge   (bri<u>dge</u> "j") May be used only after a single vowel which does not say its name.

oe   (t<u>oe</u> "ō")

gh   (<u>gh</u>ost "g")

ti	(na <u>ti</u>on "sh") (See page 4 in the Child's Notebook.)
si	(ses <u>si</u>on "sh," vi <u>si</u>on "zh")
ci	(fa <u>ci</u>al "sh")

ough	<u>though</u>	"ō"
	<u>through</u>	"o͞o"
	<u>rough</u>	"ŭf"
	<u>cough</u>	"ŏf"
	<u>thought</u>	"aw"
	<u>bough</u>	"ow"

The following phonograms are not listed on the 70 phonogram cards. They are to be taught in Grade VI and above. They may be introduced separately at an earlier time if they are needed.

eu   (<u>Eu</u> r<u>o</u>p<u>e</u> "ū")

pn   (<u>pneu</u> m<u>o</u> ni å "n") kn, gn, pn are alike in sound.

rh   (<u>rh</u>i noc <u>er</u> os "r")

q̇u   (mos q̇<u>u</u>i t<u>o</u> "k")

x̣   (x̣<u>y</u> l<u>o</u> <u>phone</u> "z")

Spelling Rules

For convenient reference the rules given in the Teacher's Notes about the first seven pages of the Child's Notebook are listed below in the same order. Additional useful spelling rules are appended and numbered for reference.

Almost no rule is absolute. It is well to make this clear and to say that we shall all be on the lookout for words that do not conform to the rules. Such words can be readily learned and a little drill is needed for them. In the whole Ayres list of a thousand words which are given in Chapter Six less than fifty have any part which does not agree with the sounds on the phonogram cards or with these rules of spelling. However all these rules hold true often enough to be very helpful. It makes a good and useful game to have the children "discover" words where the rules do not apply. That way they make an impression not quickly forgotten. Finding soccer where we drop the sound of the second c, or facade where c says "s" and is not followed by e, i or y, are examples.

Rule 1. q is always written with 2 letters, qu, when we say "kw." The u is not considered a vowel here. (See Page 1 of the Notebook.)

Rule 2. When c by itself has a sound, (not part of a two-letter phonogram) it always says "s" if followed by e, i or y (cent, city, cyclone). If not followed by one of these letters its sound is "k," (cat, claw, cyclone). This is true in spelling and in reading. (See Page 1 of the Notebook.)

Rule 3. When g has a sound by itself it can say "j" only when followed by e, i or y. When followed by any other letter it says "g." (Get, girl and give prove that there are a few exceptions to this rule.) In spelling, if you use g to say "j" it must be followed by e, i or y—as in pigeon, religious. (See Page 1 of the Notebook.)

Rule 4. Vowels a, e, o, u usually say "ā," "ē," "ō," "ū," at the end of a syllable. This is one of but three ways a vowel may say ā, ē, ī, ō or ū. (See Page 1 of the Notebook.)

Rule 5. i and y can say "ī" at the end of a syllable but usually they say "ĭ." This is shown at the end of the second syllable of both Indĭan and babȳ.

Rule 6. y, not i, is used at the end of an English word. (Taxi is short for taxicab and macaroni is an Italian word. Words like these should be explained when they are met.) (See Page 1 of the Notebook.)

Rule 7. There are five kinds of silent e. (See Page 1 of the Child's Notebook.) These five silent e's are indicated by special markings in this book, as shown at the bottom of Page 1. The notes to teachers for this page explain these five kinds of silent e's.

Rule 8. or may say "er" when w comes before the or, as in work. (See Page 2 of Notebook.)

Rule 9. After c we use ei.

If we say "ā" we can use ei, but never ie. In the list of exceptions we use ei. In all other words using ie or ei we use ie. (See Page 3 of Notebook.)

Rule 10. sh is used at the beginning of a word and at the end of a syllable (she, finish) but except in the ending ship (friendship) not at the beginning of any syllable after the first one. (See Page 4 of Notebook.)

Rule 11. ti, si, ci are the spellings most frequently used to say "sh" at the beginning of a second or subsequent syllable. (See Page 4 of Notebook.)

Rule 12. si is used to say "sh" when the syllable before it ends in an s (ses sion), and when the base word has an s where the base word changes (tense, ten sion). (See Page 4 of Notebook.)

Rule 13. si (not ti or ci) can also say "zh," as in division.

Rule 14. Words of one syllable (like hop) ending in one consonant, which have only one vowel before this last consonant, always double the last consonant before adding an ending that begins with a vowel. (See Page 5 of Notebook.)

Rule 15. Words of two syllables, like begin, where the second syllable gin is like hop, having one consonant at the end and one vowel before it, also double this last consonant before adding an ending that begins with a vowel, if the accent is on the second syllable. (See Page 5 of Notebook.)

Rule 16. Words ending with one of the five kinds of silent e's drop the e when adding an ending that begins with a vowel. (When the ending does not begin with an e, i or y the silent e is retained so that g can say "j" as in changeable, or so the c can say "s" in noticeable.) (See Page 6 of Notebook.)

Rule 17. In English we often double l, f, s following a single vowel at the end of a word of one syllable, as in will, off, glass, roll. Children must learn where these come and then they must learn words like recess, distaff, egg and add, when they meet them.

Rule 18. ay is used to say "ā" at the end of a word, rather than a alone, except for the article a.

Rule 19. A vowel may say its name if it is followed by two consonants (find, old).

Rule 20. s never follows x. There is an s sound in x (ks).

Rule 21. All, written alone, has double l, but written with another syllable only one l is used: al so, al most.

Rule 22. When till and full are added to another syllable we drop one l: un til, beau ti ful.

Rule 23. dge may be used only after a single vowel which does not say its name, as in bridge.

Rule 24. When adding an ending to a word that ends with a y that has a sound alone, change the y to i unless the ending is ing: carry is changed to carried and carries but in carrying we keep the y. In English we almost never have an i follow i. In the words played, boys, we do not change the y since it is ay and oy, and not y alone for its sound.

Rule 25. ck may be used only after a single vowel when it does not say its name, and only at the end of a syllable, or at the end of a base word.

Rule 26. Words which are the individual names or titles of people, of places, of books, of days and months, etc., are capitalized. (Mary, Honolulu, Amazon River, Bible, Monday, July)

Rule 27. s is never used to say "z" at the beginning of a base word, (zero).

Rule 28. ed says "d" or "t" at the end of any word except one ending in a "d" or "t" sound (liv*ed*, jump*ed*). If a base word ends in the sound "d" or "t" adding ed makes another syllable which says "ed" (sid *ed*, part *ed*)

CHAPTER VI

The Application of the Phonograms and the Rules

THIS CHAPTER gives children the needed training in the use of what
they have been learning about writing the sounds, and about the rules
of spelling. A thousand words most commonly used in English are
taken from the "Ayres List" from *Measuring Scale for Ability in Spelling*
by Leonard P. Ayres.* The words are dictated by the teacher, in the
order given. The child says only the first phonogram of a one-syllable
word and writes it. As he writes that sound he says the next one, and so
on until he finishes the word. For words of more than one syllable, he
says the first syllable and starts to write it. Before he finishes writing it,
he says the next syllable, writes it and so on. This eliminates saying the
whole word before starting to write. He does not say the names of the
letters unless the sound and the name are the same. He should say
only the sound of the phonogram. This permits the child to write
about as fast as he can speak distinctly.

The dictionary has been followed as closely as possible for sounds
for teaching spelling. I use but three sounds each for a, o and u, and
two sounds each for e, i and y. This promotes far more accurate speaking than usually can be found in our schools.

In pronouncing each syllable before he writes it the child should

---

* Educational Testing Service, Princeton, N. J.

stress the vowel wherever possible in order to be in agreement with the spelling. In normal speaking or reading, the rhythm of speech and sentence accent, as well as word accent, reduces very naturally many of such stressed vowels to their dictionary pronunciation. The dictionary states that a monosyllable word (or a syllable of a longer word) when pronounced alone, always stresses the vowel. This conforms to the spelling but sometimes differs slightly from the proper pronunciation when it is spoken in context. This stressing of vowel sounds makes spelling much more phonetic and easy to learn. WEBSTER'S COLLEGIATE DICTIONARY, the 1953 edition, explains on page ix the correct variations in pronouncing words in different contexts and uses.

The teacher dictates the whole word as spoken in normal conversation (not by syllables) to the children. She then gives a sentence containing the word. The teacher's sentences can restate useful facts such as how the children should sit or hold their pencil, form letters, facts about how the language works, etc. She can tell the children how good they are at reasoning, studying, playing, and even insert philosophical ideas about learning. They need not be dull, unimaginative sentences, but they should be short, and models of English. They serve as a standard for the type of sentences she wants from the children when their turn comes to use the word in a sentence.

Whenever a spelling rule accounts for the spelling of a word, it is explained with that word. These rules are not so much to be memorized as they are to be taught as facts about the language which the teacher helps the children to discover. In this way the children sense the meaning of each rule instead of having a mere parroted memorizing of it, a most important difference.

The following five items explain the simple markings of the words of the Ayres list which are used to impress on the children how the rules and phonograms actually work.

1) A vowel is underlined at the end of a syllable when it says its name.

m<u>e</u>

<u>o</u> pen

J<u>u</u> l<u>y</u>

(Spelling Rule 5 states that i and y usually say "ī" at the end of a syllable. Where this is true i and y are not underlined — fam i ly.)

2) Phonograms of two or more letters are underlined.

<u>th</u>in

bri<u>dge</u>

<u>eigh</u>t

3) Silent letters and phonograms when their sound is one not given on the phonogram cards, have a double line under them.

ha<u>l</u>f (We say "haf" but write half.)

fri<u>e</u>nd (ĕ is not one of the sounds on card 57 for ie.)

The silent e at the end of a base word is one of five different kinds and each kind is marked as shown below. All except the first kind have a number below to show which kind it is. (See the teacher's notes for page 1 of the Notebook.)

t<u>im</u>e

ha<u>ve</u>₂   bl<u>ue</u>₂

chan<u>ce</u>₃   char<u>ge</u>₃

lit tl<u>e</u>₄

ar<u>e</u>₅

4) Numbers are placed above a phonogram when its sound is not the first sound given on its card. (Except where a line is used under a vowel which says its name at the end of a syllable.)

d<u>o</u>³   l<u>ow</u>²

w<u>a</u><u>s</u>³²   y<u>ou</u>³

p<u>u</u>t³   c<u>ou</u>n try⁴

<u>though</u>t⁵

b<u>ough</u>⁶

5) Some words are bracketed together. In such cases the first word
is in the Ayres list. The others have been added to show (1)
the base word, or (2) several words with the same peculiarity
in spelling, or (3) how some words are said alike but use different phonograms in spelling, or (4) contrast in the sounds
of two words that might easily be confused.

Techniques of Presenting the Words of the Ayres List.

These words are to be presented orally by the teacher. The children do not see these words until they write them from dictation.

The teacher says the first word "me" and gives a sentence containing me. The word is not unfamiliar. The meaning is clear and the
only problem is how to write it.

The children give the first sound "m." She writes on the board
while they write. As they start the writing of "m" they say "e" and
write e. They underline the e and the teacher points out that under
Rule 1 a, e, o, u say their names at the end of a syllable. The children
then read me aloud.

The teacher then dictates "do" and gives a sentence containing
do. The children say "d" and before finishing the writing of "d" they
say "ōō," write o, and put a 3 above it. In the initial presentation
the teacher says, "We write the letter which says 'ŏ, ō, ōō.'" They
then read "do."

All of these words are to be taught just as described above and in
the notes to the teacher regarding the first seven pages of the Child's
Notebook. First- and second-grade children will not have written in
notebooks these seven pages but will be taught the rules and facts
which these seven pages contain as these points come up in the words
of the Ayres list. They will however have their own notebooks in
which to write the words dictated from the Ayres list. The third and
upper grade children first write the seven pages of the Child's Notebook, (which they should correct until they have an exact model just
as shown in Chapter V), and they follow this with the dictated words.

After each word is written a child should read it and give a sentence containing the word. This latter may well be postponed until all the words in the day's lesson are written.

Almost all of this list of 1000 words are in the spoken or "understood" vocabulary of normal six-year-old children. Teachers should of course introduce and teach no words far beyond the easy understanding of the children in their age group. It seems silly to mention this but critics of phonics seem to assume that if the sounds of the language are taught the meaning of individual words and sentences is overlooked. Experience with our phonics is quite the reverse and such criticism quite unfounded.

Words in Sections A to H (From the Ayres List)
(Study the above techniques and the five numbered explanations of underline and number markings.)

me̲   **Rule 4.** (e says "ē" at the end of a syllable)

do̲³   The third sound on the phonogram card for o is "ōō"

and

go̲   **Rule 4.** (o says "ō" at the end of a syllable)

at

on

a̲   **Rule 4.** (a may say "ā" because it ends the syllable. In speech when the accent is not on a its sound becomes "à" as shown in the dictionary. For spelling say "ā.")

it

is̱²   (s says "z," the second sound on its card)

she   **Rule 4.** (It takes two letters to write the sound "sh.")

can

see   (We use the two letter card ee to write "ē" in see. When
         children are writing words for the first time the teacher
         tells them which phonogram the dictionary uses where
         there are several possibilities.)

run

²
the   **Rule 4.**

in

so   **Rule 4.**

no   **Rule 4.**

now   (There are two cards for the sound "ow." We use ow
         here since English words should not end with u.)

man

ten

bed

top

he   **Rule 4.**

³
you   (The third sound on the card for ou is "o͞o." You and
         thou are two of the few words that end with ou. y at
         the beginning of a word is always the consonant y. This

is important for reading only, since in translating sound there is but one phonogram given for the consonant "y.")

will   **Rule 17.** (We often double l, f, s, following a single vowel at the end of one-syllable words.)

we   **Rule 4.**

an

my   **Rules 5 and 6.** (English words do not end with i. We use y which has the sounds of i.)

up

last   (We use s, not c, since Rule 2 shows c would say "k" here.)

not

us

am

good   (The second sound for oo is "ŏŏ.")

lit tle   (Page 1 in the Notebook gives the five silent final e's. tl sound but the e is silent. Child says "lit" and writes it, then "tle" and writes it. In the spelling lesson words should be written in syllables. In writing sentences, of course, they cannot be divided.)

Using the two hands to give the kinesthetic feel of the two syllables helps here.

a go̲ **Rule 4.** (Child says "ā" and writes it, then "go" and writes it. In reading or speaking a̲go̲, the accent is on go̲ and therefore the full sound "ā" cannot be said. This deterioration in sound is caused by the rhythm of English speech which must always be taught in reading and in speech.)

o̊ld **Rule 19.** (i or o may say its name if followed by two consonants.)

bad

red

of̲ (We say "v" but write "f." Both must be learned. Put two lines under f. They indicate here that the sound we write for spelling is different from the sound in speech.)

be̲ **Rule 4.**

but

this̲ **Rule 4.**

åll The teacher tells that we use the letter that says "ă, ā, ah" when the children give the first sound of all.

Rule 17. (The third sound of a is "ah" on its phonogram card. This is a slight overtone used here for spelling.)

yo̲u̲r (yo̲u is the base word of yo̲u̲r)

yo̲u

o̲u̲t　　In the first presentation the teacher shows the ou card (which says "ow, ō, ōo, ŭ") to write the first sound of o̲u̲t.

ti̲m̲e̲　　No. 1 on page 1 of the Child's Notebook. "ī," consonant, e. We put the silent e on so the i can say "ī." Without the e the word would be T̲i̲m̲.

The child has now met the three usual ways for a vowel to say its name: 1) by ending the syllable (me),

　　　2) by having two consonants follow it (ȯld), and

　　　3) by being followed by a consonant and a silent e (time).

It follows that the o of of should say ŏ, the ŭ of bu̲t̲ should say ŭ, etc.

ma̲y̲　　**Rule 18.** (At the end of a word we use ay to say "ā" rather than a alone, except in the article a.)

in t o̲³

him

t o̲³ da̲y̲　　**Rule 18.**

lo̲²o̲k̲　　The teacher tells that we use the card that says "ōo, ŏo, ō" to say "ōo" in lo̲o̲k̲.

　　　Rule 25. (We could not use ck at the end.)

did

⌈ li̲k̲e̲　　Page 1 of the Notebook. We need the silent e so the i can say "ī."

│　　　(We must use k, not c, to say "k.")

⌊ li̲c̲e̲

six

boy   **Rule 6** shows why we would not use oi here.

book   **Rule 25.**

by   **Rule 6.**

have   Refer to the five kinds of silent e on page 1 of the Child's
          Notebook. The a says "ā" but we still need the e. English
          words do not end with v.

are   Page 1 of the Notebook. This is a silent e with no job.

had

o ver   **Rule 4.** (Page 2 of the Child's Notebook gives the spell-
          ings for "er." This er we use most often.)

must

make   Page 1 of the Notebook. The e makes the a say "ā." We
          could not use c to say "k" because we need the e so the a
          can say "ā" and the e would make a c say "s."

school   (The second sound of ch is "k.") It takes four phono-
          grams to write school.

street   It takes five phonograms to write street.

say   **Rule 18.**

come   Page 1 of the Notebook. This silent e has no job.

hand

ring   Be sure each child says ng correctly.

live   The e makes the i say "ī."

live₂   Page 1 of the Notebook. The i does not say "ī" in live₂
but we need the silent e since no English word may end
in v.

kill   **Rule 17.** (We use c at the beginning of common words
when we can. Here we cannot for it would
say "s.")

late   The e makes the a say "ā."

let

big

moth er   (Page 2 of the Notebook gives the spellings of the sound
"er." We use er more often than the other four. The dictionary says we say "ŭ" instead of "ŏ." The overtone "ŏ"
can be said in saying individual syllables for spelling. The
rhythm when saying the syllables together causes the
lower sound "ŭ.")

three

land

cold   **Rule 19.**

hot

hat

child   **Rule 19.**

ice   The e makes the i say "ī."
Rule 2 is secondary here.

pl<u>a</u>y   **Rule 18.**

⌈ s<u>ea</u>   ee and ea (each saying "ē") show that the words have dif-

⌊ s<u>ee</u>   ferent meanings.

Section H

Do not relax nor shorten the method of presenting the following words. Follow in detail the same procedure in teaching each word as outlined at the beginning of the Ayres list.

d<u>a</u>y   **Rule 18.**

<u>ea</u>t   The teacher tells that the dictionary gives the ea card ("ē, ĕ, ā") for the ē sound in eat. The child should soon be able to give this information to the teacher when eat is dictated in subsequent lessons. Drill is necessary on such words.

sit

lot

box   (x = "ks" in sound)

b<u>e</u> lo<u>ng</u>   **Rule 4.**

⌈ d<u>o͞o</u>r   (door and floor are the only words in *The Ayres list* in which oo says "ō." In all other words oo will say "o͞o" or

⌊ fl<u>o͞o</u>r   "o͝o."

yes

lo͝w

soft

stand

y<u>ar</u>d

bri<u>ng</u>

tell   **Rule 17.**

f<u>i̯ve</u>   (The e makes the i say "ī." This is its primary job.)

b³all   **Rule 17** (The third sound for a is "ah" as shown on its phonogram card and on page 1 of the Note-book. This is a slight overtone here for spelling.)

l<u>aw</u>   (We use aw, not au, at the end of a word since u should not end a word.)

ask   (k, not ck, is used because a consonant sits before. ck can be used only after a single vowel which does not say its name.)

⎡ just   (We must write j here, for g would say "g" since it is not
⎣ gust   followed by e, i or y.)

w<u>ay</u>   **Rule 18.**

get

h<u>ome</u>   The e makes the o say "ō."

mu<u>ch</u>

cȧll   **Rule 17.**

lo̱ng

love̱   The e is needed since no English word may end in v.

then

house̱   The ou sound in <u>house</u> is from the card ou (which says
          "ow, ō, ōō, ŭ"). The e has no job.

year   (<u>Year</u> takes three phonogram cards.)

tȯ

I   (We always write a capital I because this word stands for
          one's own name: Mary, John, etc. This is one of the few
          exceptions to Rule 6.)

aṡ

send

one   (Spell <u>one</u> by saying the names of the letters if necessary.
          We probably once said <u>one</u> as in <u>lone</u> and <u>only</u> which
lone   mean one. Phonetically we would say "on." Since we
          say "won" (the dictionary deteriorates the sound to
a lone   "wun"), the correct spelling must be learned. <u>of</u> and <u>one</u>
          are the only words in the first grade list where sound and
haṡ   written form are not the same.)

some   The e has no job.

if

h<u>ow</u>

h<u>er</u>

²
th<u>e</u>m

²
o<u>th</u> <u>er</u>

b<u>a</u> by   (y says "ĭ." Be sure the children say "ĭ." To write babies
we change the y of baby to i and add es.)

well   Rule 17.

<u>a</u> b<u>ou</u>t

⌈ men

⌊ man

f<u>or</u>

⌈ ran

⌊ run

^{3 2}
wa̱s   (The first time was is sounded and written the teacher
tells phonograms to use. The next time the children will
tell which phonograms we write.)

²
<u>th</u>at

²
hi<u>s</u>

led

lay   **Rule 18.**

(This is the point of *minimum* accomplishment in a first grade. However, the class as a whole should reach this point by November and start reading from pre-primers. See report given on pages 218 and 219.)

Section I

The five kinds of silent e found on Page 1 of the Notebook will no longer have a notation after them. They will be underlined and numbered as they are on Page 1 of the Notebook.

nine

face   (c can be used since we put an e after it. The children must learn to write c in this word. Drill is necessary.)

miss   **Rule 17.**

ride

tree

sick   **Rule 25.** (ck is used here after a single vowel.)

got

north

white   (wh has no sound but air can be felt on the hand held before the lips. Ask children to blow air out and feel it on their hands. "white" not wite.)

spent

foot

blọ̄w

block

spriṇg

riv er   (The child says "riv" and writes it, if he can, without
           sounding the individual sounds. Before finishing the
           writing of riv he says er and writes that.)

plant

cut

song

sing

sang

sung

win ter

stone

free

lake

lace

page

nice

end

făll   Rule 17.

f<u>ee</u>t

went

ba<u>ck</u>   Rule 25.

a w<u>ay</u>

pa per

pŭt   We use the u card (which says "ŭ, ū, o͞o.")

<u>ea</u>ch

s<u>oo</u>n

c<u>a</u>m<u>e</u>

Sun d<u>ay</u>   Rule 26. (Sunday is the day's own name and like a child's own name, John White, must be written with a capital letter. Sunday was named for the sun.)

sho̅w

Mon d<u>ay</u>   Rule 26. (Monday is the day's own name and must be written with a capital letter. Monday was named for the moon.)

m<u>oo</u>n

yet

find   Rule 19.

give₂

new   ew says "ū."

let ter

take

Mr. = Mister   In Mr. we left out 4 letters and put a period at the
               end. When we leave out letters of a single word and
               put a period at the end we call this an abbreviation.
               Rule 26. Mr. is always written with a man's name
               (Mr. Brown).

af ter

thing

what   (Be sure children do not say "watt" for "what."

than

its   (Its is used as we use her or his.)

it's = It is The apostrophe is used in place of the i of is. When we
            put words together and leave out some letters, we put in
            an apostrophe where letters are omitted. This is a con-
            traction.

ver y   The e says "ĕ." Three phonograms are needed to write
         ver. y says "ĭ."

<u>or</u>

th<u>a</u>nk　　(We say "thangk" but for spelling say "th," "ă," "n," "k.")

d<u>ea</u>r

west

s$\overset{2}{o}$ld　　Rule 19.

t$\overset{2}{o}$ld　　Rule 19.

best

f<u>or</u>m

f<u>a</u>r

g<u>a</u>v<u>e</u>

<u>a</u> l<u>i</u>ke

add　　(Learn to double the d. Addition needs both d's.)

Section J

sev en

f<u>or</u> get

hap py　　(y says "ĭ.")

n<u>oo</u>n

think

sis ter

cast

card

south

deep

in side

blue

póst   Rule 19.

town

stay

grand

out side

dark

band

game

boat

rest

east

son   Sound ŏ for spelling.

sun

help

hard

race

cov er

fire   (Be sure the children say "r" and do not say "fi er.")
              These words have but one syllable.

wire

tire

age

gŏld   **Rule 19.**

read   (a book)

rĕad   (a book)

red

fine

can not

May Rule 26.

may

line

left

ship

train

saw

pay

large₃

near

down

why   (Not "wy")

bill

wȧnt

girl   (Page 2 in Child's Notebook.)

part

still

pl**a**ce

re p**o**rt

nev **er**

f**ou**nd

s**i**de

k**i**nd   Rule 19.

l**i**fe

h**ere**

c**ar**

w**or**d   **Rule 8.** (Page 2 of the Notebook.)

ev **er** y   **Rule 5.**

un **der**

m**o**st   **Rule 19.**

m**a**de

s**ai**d   (Say ā when writing. Its base word is say. We say "sed"
       in speaking. Both the writing and the reading must be
       learned since the two are different.)

s**ay**

w**or**k   **Rule 8.** (Page 2 of the Notebook.)

our

more

when

from

form

wind

²wind   (the clock) **Rule 19.**

print

air

fill   **Rule 17.**

a long

lost

name

room

hope

same

glad

wi<u>th</u>²

m<u>i</u>n<u>e</u>

At this point we should discuss base words and derivatives. Many words are derived from "base" words and it is always important for word meaning, grammar and a grasp of how the language is formed that the base word be taught with each derived word. For example, please is the base word for pleasant, pleasure, displease, etc. It is important also that the children learn that, although many words contain the spellings of shorter words which are not related in meaning —this fact is a mere coincidence which they should ignore. The phonics teaching now being used in many schools classifies rhyming words like ill, will, bill, fill, kill, mill, etc., as word families. This is wrong. They are not families but completely unrelated words.

Section K

b<u>e</u> c<u>a</u>m<u>e</u>

bro<u>th</u>² er

r<u>ai</u>n

k<u>ee</u>p

st<u>a</u>rt

m<u>ai</u>l

m<u>a</u>l<u>e</u>

f<u>e</u> m<u>a</u>l<u>e</u>

eye

(eye is not phonetic. The picture gives the spelling and the meaning of eye. This is the only word in *The Ayres list* where a picture is helpful in learning the spelling of a word.

I

glass

par ty   y says "ī."

up on

two

(For spelling say the sounds of the three letters we write. Two is not phonetic. We probably once said "two" sounding the "w" as we still do in twin and twice.)

twin

twice

they

would   (Sound as it is written for spelling. We say wŏod.)

an y   (Sound "ă" as it is written for spelling. We say "ĕ" in normal speech and in reading.)

man y

could   (Sound the 4 sounds as they are written for spelling. We say cŏod.)

should   (Sound the 4 sounds as they are written for spelling. We say shŏod.)

cit y

on ly   (The base word is one.)

where₅   (Not wear)

week

weak

first   (Page 2 in the Notebook.)

sent

cent

mile

seem   (Base word is see.)

see

e ven

with out

af ter noon

Fri day   **Rule 26.** (Friday was named for Frigga, the wife of Odin, in Norse Myth.)

hour   (For spelling pronounce the h as it is written. Compare meaning with our.)

our

wīfe

stāte

Ju ly   Rule 26.

hĕad

sto ry

o pen

short

la dy   (y says "ī.")

reach

bet ter

wā ter

round

cost

prīce

be come₅

class   Rule 17.

horse₅

care

try

move₂

de lay   Rule 18.

pound

be hind   Rule 19.

a round

burn   (Page 2 of the Notebook.)

camp

bear

bare

clear

clean

spell

poor

fin ish

hurt   (Page 2 of the Notebook.)

may be   (It may be—is the meaning.)

a cross   **Rule 17.**

tŏ night   (We use three letters to say "ī.")

tenth

sir   (Page 2 of the Notebook.)

these

those

club

seen   (Base word is see.)

see

felt

fŭll   **Rule 17.**

fail

set

stamp

light

com ing   (Page 6 of the Notebook.)

come

cent   (Compare meaning with sent.)

sent

night

pass   **Rule 17.**

shut

eas y   (Page 6 of the Notebook.)

ease.5

Section L

catch   (Pronounce the "t" in writing)

black   **Rule 25.**

warm

un less   **Rule 17.**

cloth ing   (Page 6 of the Notebook.)

clothe

be gan

be gin

be gun

a ble₄

gone₅

go

done₅   (Say ŏ for writing.)

do

suit   (ui says "ū.")

track   Rule 25.

watch   (Pronounce t, in writing.)

dash

fell   Rule 17.

fight

buy   (Sound "ŭ" in writing. Discuss meaning.)

by

stop

walk   (Sound as written for spelling. We say "wăk," "tăk," "băk.")

talk

balk

grant

soap   This oa may be taught as the "ō" in the key word boat.

news

new

small   Rule 17.

war

sum mer

a bove

ex press   Rule 20.

turn   (Page 2 of the Notebook.)

les son

half   (Sound 1, for spelling. We say "haf.")

fa ther

an y thing   (Say ă in writing.)

ta ble

high

talk   (Sound 1 in writing.)

June   Rule 26.

right

write

wrote

date

road

rode

ride

March   Rule 26.

march

next

in deed

four

her self

pow er

wish

be cause

w**or**ld   (Page 2 of the Notebook.)

c**oun** try

> m**ee**t
>
> m**ea**t

an o**th** **er**

trip

list

p**e o pl**e   (Children enjoy saying 3 syllables for writing. We say
"p**e** pl**e**")

ev **er**

held

chur**ch**   (Page 2 of the Notebook.)

> on**ce**   (Base word is one. Neither one nor once is phonetic. We
> say "won**ce**" and "won.")
>
> one

own

b**e** f**or**e

> kn**o**w
>
> n**o**

were₅

where₅   (These four words have the same last three letters but
          they are not all said alike. Each is phonetic, however.)

there₅

here

dead

leave₂

ear ly   (Page 2 in the Notebook.)

close

close

flow er

flour   (The last sound is "r," not er.)

noth ing

ground

lead   (the way)

led   (the way)

lead   (pencil)

such

man y   (Say "ă," when writing. We say "men y.")

morn ing

how ev er

mind   Rule 19.

shall   Rule 17.

a lone

or der

third   (Page 2 of the Notebook.)

push

point

with in

done₅

do

gone₅

go

body   (y says "ĭ.")

(This is the point of *minimum* accomplishment in a second grade, but the class, by February, should be taught as far as Section P on page 182. See report on pages 220 and 221.)

Note to teachers. For spelling ask the children to say polysyllable words in syllables. When the word is written, ask them to read it in syllables and then read it again as a word in proper English rhythm.

By now Rules 4, 5, 6, 7, 8, 17, 18, 19, 25 should be understood. They will no longer be noted.

Section M

trust

ex trā³

dress

bē sīde

tēach

hap pen

bē gun

col lect   (We often have the 2 sounds "c" and "t" at the end of a word: direct, elect, protect. Sound each carefully.)

fīle

prō vīde

sīght

stoŏd²

fix

b**or**n

g**o**es   (Learn: Add **es** to go, do and Tu to make goes, does
          and Tuesday.)

go

d**oes**

d**o**

T**ue**s d**ay**

h**o**ld

drill

ar my

pr**e**t ty   (Say ĕ for writing only. We say "prit ty.")

st**ole**

in c**ome**

b**ou**ght

paid   p**ay**   (The base words are pay, lay and say. We change the
                 form of these words and do not add ed to the base
laid   l**ay**   words.)

s**ai**d   s**ay**   (We write "said" but we say "sed." Both must be
                 learned.)

en ter

rail road (The rails are on the road.)

un a ble

tick et

ac count We cannot say ā here. When the sound is definitely ă the
vowel is followed by a consonant. (ăr rive, ăf fect, ăp pear)

driv en

re al

re cov er

moun tain (Sound it as it is written for spelling. We say "moun
ten.")

steam er

speak

past

might

be gin

con tract

deal

al̊ mȯst   **Rule 21.**

all̊

brou̇ght

less

e̲ vent

off

of̰

truḛ₂

to̲o̲k

a̲ ga̲in   (Sound it as it is written for spelling. We say "a̲ gen."
          The British say it as it is written.)

in fo̲rm

bo̊t̲h̲

hea̲r̲t̲   (Not phonetic. We say "hart" but write heart. The doc-
          tor listens to your heart with his ear.)

mont̲h̲

chi̲l dren

chi̊l̲d

bu̇ ild   (We say "bild.")

bu̇ ilt

un der stand

fol low

charge₃

says   (Sound it as it is written for spelling. We say "sĕs.")

say

mem ber

case

while   (Not "wile.")

al so   Rule 21.

re turn   (Page 2 in Notebook.)

those

these

of fice₃

great

Miss

miss

wh**o** (Sound it as written for spelling. We say "ho.")

d**ied** (The e serves two functions: ie says "ī" and ed says "d.")

d**ie** (Page 3 in the Notebook.)

ch**ange** (The e makes the a say "ā" even though there are two consonants between. The e also permits the g to say "j" but this is a secondary job.)

w**ire**

f**ew** (ew says "ŭ.")

ple**ase**₅

pic t**ure**

mon e**y** (ey says "ĭ.")

r**ea**d y

o mit

an y w**ay** (Sound as it is written for spelling.)

an y

w**ay**

Section N

ex cept   (c followed by e, i or y may follow x. See Rule 20.)

⎡ a̲unt   (Sound as written for spelling.)

⎣ ant

cap t̲ure̲

⎡ w̲rote̲

⎣ w̲rite̲

else̲⁵

bridge   Rule 23.

of fe̲r

suf fe̲r

⎡ bu̇¹ ilt

⎣ bu̇¹ ild

cen te̲r

front

r̲u̲le̲   (Say ū for spelling.)

cȧ¹r ry

chain

death

learn   (Page 2 in the Notebook.)

won der

tire

pair   (two)

pear   (eat)

pare   (cut)

check

prove

heard   (Page 2 in the Notebook.)

hear

in spect

it self

al ways   Rule 21.

some thing

write

wrote

ex pect   Rule 20.

ne͟ed

²th͟us

wo͟ man	(Sound as written for spelling. Came from wife man.
wo͟ men	Then say "wo͞²om an" and "wim en.")

yo͞u͟ng⁴

fa͟ir
fare

dol la͟r

eve ni͟ng
eve

plan

bro͟ke

fe͟el

sure	(s here says "sh" in normal speech. Sound "s" for writ-
	ing.)
su͟g a͟r³	

le͝ast

sŏr¹ ry

press

⎡ God   Rule 26.

⎣ god

te͝ach͟ er͟

N͟o͟ vem ber͟   Rule 26. This is the ninth month of the old
                          Roman year. (novem or nine)

sub ject

A͟ pril   Rule 26.

his t͟o͟ ry

cau͟s̆e²₅

stud y

him self

mat te͟r͟

u͟s̆e²

th͟ou͟g͟ht⁵

pe͟r͟ son

nor   (Explain the use of nor and or.)

or

Jan u a ry   **Rule 26.** (We say "Jan u ĕr y." Named for Roman god, Janus.)

mean

vote

court

cop y

act

been   (Sound as it is written for spelling. We say "bin." The British say "been." Base word is be.)

be

yes ter day

a mong

ques tion   (Sound as it is written for spelling. We say "ch" here for ti.)

quest

doc tor

hear

si̱ẕe̱   Few words use z except at the beginning of a base word. Size, dozen, organize, citizen are about the only ones in the first 1000 words.

De̱ cem be̱r   **Rule 26.** (This was the tenth month of the Roman calendar. Decem means ten)

doz en

the̱re̲₅

tax

num be̱r

Oc to̱ be̱r   **Rule 26.** (The eighth month of the Roman calendar. Octo means eight.)

rea s̱on

fif̱ṯẖ

Section O

eight

a̱te̱

a̱ fra̱id

un cle̲₄

ra̱ṯẖ er̲

com fo̱rt

e lect

a board   (This is the "ō" we use in boat. The use of the word
            boat should come to distinguish this spelling of "ō"
            from the several others.)

jail

shed

re tire

re fuse

dis trict

re strain

roy al

ob jec tion   (Page 4 of the Notebook.)

ob ject

pleas ure   (Comes from please.)

meas ure

treas ure

na vy

fourth

four

pop u la tion   (Page 4 of the Notebook.)

prop er

judge   Rule 23.

weath er   The first sounds of these two words are different.

wheth er

worth   (Page 2 of the Notebook.)

con tain

fig ure

sud den

for ty   (Why the our is changed to or in forty is not obvious.
              The spelling must be learned.)

four

fourth

four teen

in stead

throw

threw

per son al

ev er y thing

rate

chief   **Rule 9.** (Page 3 of the Notebook.)

per fect

sec ond

slide

far ther

du ty

in tend

com pan y

quite

quit

qui et

knew

know

re main

di rect

ap pear

lib er ty

e nough

fact

board   (We use the ō of boat.)

Sep tem ber

sta tion   (Page 4 of the Notebook.)

at tend

be tween

pub lic   (We seldom use c at the end of a word.)

mu sic

pic nic   When adding ing we use ck to keep the "k" sound. (pic-nick ing)

friend   (ie says "ĕ") Page 3 of the Notebook

dur ing

en dure

through

po lice   (The children will enjoy saying this as it is written for spelling. We say "po lece.")

un til   **Rule 22.**

mad am

tru ly   (Learn to drop the e of true when writing truly. The e is used at the end of true because we do not end words with true   a single u. In truly it is no longer needed, and it is dropped even though the ending does not begin with a vowel.)

whole   (Sound as it is written for spelling.)

hole

ad dress

re quest

raise

Au gust

Tues day (Learn—Add es to Tu, go and do.)

goes

does

struck

get̠ ting   (Page 5 in the Notebook.)

get

dȯn't = dȯ not   (The apostrophe shows where a letter has been
left out. Don't is a contraction. We contracted
two words into one word.)

Thurs day   (Page 2 in the Notebook) (Thursday is Thor's day.)

Sat ur day   (Saturday is Saturn's day.)

Ninety-five per cent of these words are strictly phonetic.

(This is the point of *minimum* accomplishment in a third grade, but
many third grades finish the Ayres list through page 210.)

Section P

spend

en joy

aw ful   Rule 22.

awe

u su al

com plaint

au to

va ca tion

bea u ti fŭl³   (Sound as it is written for spelling. We say "bu
                   ti ful.")

bea u ty

flight

trav el

rap id   (This word is said as its meaning indicates. There is not
           time for a double p sound.)

re pair

trŏu⁴ ble ₌₄

dŏu⁴ ble ₌₄

en trance₃

im por tance₃

im por tant

car ried   Rule 24. (The ie says "ī" and ed says "d." The e has two
                       functions.)

car ry   (y says "ĭ.")

loss

for tune

em pire

may or

wait

beg

de gree

pris on

en gine

vis it

guest   (The gu go together as do qu. The u has no sound. In this case if the g were next to the e it could say "j.")

guess

de part ment

ob tain

fam i ly

an i mal

fa vor

Mrs. = Mis tress   (The period means that some letters of the word are not written. Mrs. is an abbreviation for which we say "Mis is" in speaking.)

Mr. = Mis ter   (Here we chose the first and last letters for the abbreviation.)

Miss   (Needs no period since the whole word is written.)

hus band (A husband gives his wife a band ring.)

a mount

hu man

vi ew   (The dictionary gives "vū." Sound the ĭ for spelling.)

e lec tion   (The t of elect went over to form ti.)

e lect

clerk

though

o'clock   (Means "of the clock." f and the are left out in this contraction of three words to a word of two syllables.)

sup port

does   (Add es to do and go to make does and goes.)

goes

re gard

es cape

since

which   (Not witch)

length   (Sound ng correctly.)

long

strength

strong

de stroy

news pa per

daugh ter   (Few words use augh, so this phonogram was not put on a card. Learn.)

naugh ty

caught

taught

an swer   (Sound the w when writing until the spelling is learned.)

re ply

o blige   (We would not use dge here since we say "ī.")

sail

sale

cit ies   **Rule 24.** (Change the y of city to i and add es. The ie says "ī.")

cit y

known

know

sev er al

de sire

near ly

Section Q

some times

de clare

en gage

fi nal

ter ri ble

sur prise (Page 2 in the Notebook.)

pe ri od

ad di tion

em ploy

prop er ty

se lect

con nec tion

con nect

firm   (Page 2 in the Notebook.)

re gion   (gi says "j." Without the i the last syllable would say "gon."

re li gion

con vict

pri vate₅   (The ă deteriorates to "ĭ" in normal speech according to the dictionary.)

com mand

de bate

crowd

fac to ry

pub lish Rule 10.

rep re sent

term   (Page 2 in the Notebook.)

sec tion

rel a tive₂

re late

prog ress

pro gress

en tire

pres i dent

pre side

meas ure

fa mous   (ous means full of; famous means <u>full</u> <u>of</u> fame.)

fame

serve₂   (Page 2 in the Notebook.)

es tate

re mem ber

ei ther   (Page 3 in the Notebook.)

ef fort

im por tant

im por tance₃

due₂

dew

in clude

run ning   (Page 5 in the Notebook. The double n in running
                  is not the same as the two l's in allow. The double n
run   in running is a reasoned one which the child must
                  remember to do.)

al low

po si tion

field   (Page 3 in the Notebook.)

ledge   **Rule 23.**

claim

pri ma ry

re sult

Sat ur day (Page 2 in the Notebook.)

ap point

in for ma tion

whom   (Sound as written for spelling. We say "hom.")

who

ar rest

them selves   (Learn: Change "f" of self to "v" and add es.)

self

calves   (Sound the 1 for spelling.)

calf

halves   (Sound the 1 for spelling.

half

spe cial   (e says "ĕ" here. Page 4 in the Notebook.)

es pe cial ly

wo men   (Sound as written for spelling.)

wo man

pres ent

pre sent

ac tion

act

jus tice

just

gen tle man

gen tle

en clo̱s̱e̱

a̲ w̲a̲it

sup po̱s̱e̱

won de̱r fu̱l   Rule 22.

di rec t̲ion

for w̲a̲rd

ba̲c̲k w̲a̲rd

to w̲a̲rd   (Sound as written for spelling, and then say "to̱ e̱rd" for speech.)

a̲l t̲ho̱ugh   Rule 21.

prompt   (Sound p and t carefully.)

at tempt

who̱s̱e   (Sound as written and then say "ho̱s̱.")

who̱

st̲a̲te̱ ment

st̲a̲te̱

pe̱r haps

the̱ir   (Page 3 in the Notebook.)

the̱y̲

im pris on

writ ten (Page 5 in the Notebook. Think of the archaic form
  writ as the base word.)
writ

ar range (The first a says "ă." The second ă has 2 separate consonants between it and the silent e.)

(This is the point of *minimum* accomplishment for every child in a fourth grade.)

Section R

fore noon (before noon)

be fore

lose

loose (Learn: "loose tooth." Both words use oo to say "ōō.")

loss

com bin a tion

com bine

av en ue

neigh bor

weigh

wear

en ter tain

sal a ry

vis² i tor

vis² it

pub li ca tion

ma¹ chine³   (Sound as written for spelling. Then read "mă shēn.")

en gine₅

to ward   (Sound as written for spelling. Then read "to erd.")

suc cess

drown

a dopt

se cure

hon or   (Sound the h for spelling.)

prom ise₅

wreck

pre pare

ves sel

bu̲s y [2]   (Sound as written for spelling and then read "bis y.")

pre̲ fer̲

pref er ence [3] (This does not follow Rule 15. The accent changes.)

il lus tra̲te̲

il lus tra̲ tion

dif fer̲ ent

dif fer̲

ob ject

pro̲ vi si̲on [2]   Rule 13.

ac cord ing

al re̲ad y [3] [2]   Rule 21.

at ten tion

ed u̲ ca̲ tion

di rec to̲r

di rect

pu̲r pose̲ [5]   (Page 2 in the Notebook.)

com mon

di a mond

to geth er

con ven tion

in crease₅

man ner

fea ture

ar ti cle₄

serv ice₃ (Page 6 in the Notebook.)

serve₂

in jure

in ju ry

ef fect

dis trib ute

gen er al

to mor row

con sid er

a gainst   (Sound as written for spelling. Then read "à genst.")

a gain   (Sound as written for spelling. Then read "à gen.")

gain

com plete

search   (Page 2 in the Notebook.)

treas ure

pop u lar

Christ mas   (The Mass of Christ. Sound t for spelling.)

Christ   Rules 19 and 26.

in ter est

Section S

of ten   (Sound t for spelling. Then say "of en.")

stopped   (Page 5 in the Notebook.)

stop

mo tion

the a ter   (Be sure to accent the 1st syllable in speech: the' a ter.)

im prove ment

im prove

⎡ cen tu̱ ry

⎣ cent

to̱ tal

men t̲ion

¹
ar ri̲v̲e̲

sup pl̲y

as sist

dif fe̲r ence̲₃

⎡ ex am in a̲ t̲ion   (Sound as written for spelling. We say "eg zam
                        in a tion.")
⎣ ex am ine̲₅

pa̲r tic u̱ la̲r

af fa̲ir

⎡   ²
  co̱u̲rse̲₅

⎣ co̲arse̲₅

      ²
nei̲ t̲he̲r   (Page 3 in the Notebook.)

lo̱ cal

⎡   ¹
  ma̱r ri a̲g̲e̲   (Sound in 3 syllables for spelling. Then say "măr ige̲₃.")

⎣   ¹
  ma̱r ry

căr ri age̲   (Sound as written for spelling. Then say "căr ige.")

căr ry

fu̲r the̲r   (Page 2 in the Notebook.)

se̲ ri o̲us

dou̲b̲t   (Sound b for spelling.)

con di t̲ion

gov e̲rn ment

gov e̲rn

o̲ pin i̲on   (In these 7 words i uses the consonant sound of y.
             Since i and y are sounded alike as vowels, i with a
on i̲on   consonant sound of y is not too surprising.)

ŭn i̲on

fa̋ mil i̲a̲r

be̲ hav i̲o̲r   (Page 6 in the Notebook.)

com pan i̲on

mil l̲i̲on

be̲ lie̲ve̲   .(Page 3 in the Notebook.)

sys tem

pos si ble̲

pos si bly

piece₃   (Page 3 in the Notebook.)

peace₃

cer tain   (Page 2 in the Notebook.)

wit ness

in ves ti gate

there fore

be fore

too   Means: 1) also; 2) more than enough.

two

to

pleas ant

please₅

Section T

guess   (gu are together for the sound "g.")

guest

cir cu lar   (Page 2 in the Notebook.)

cir cle₄

ar gu ment   (Learn to drop the e of argue. We need the e in argue,
              only because a u should not end a word.)

ar gue ₂

vol ume

or gan ize

sum mon

of fi cial   (Page 4 in the Notebook.)

of fi cer

of fice ₃

vic tim

es ti mate

ac ci dent

in vi ta tion

in vite

ac cept

im pos si ble ₄

con cern

as <u>so</u> ci <u>ate</u>   (Page 4 in the Notebook. ci says "sh," and since it
has no other vowel as in <u>official</u>, the i is sounded. ci
here says "<u>shĭ</u>.")

<u>au</u> t<u>o</u> m<u>o</u> bil<u>e</u>₅

var̂ i <u>ou</u>s (2, 4)

var̂ y (2)

vêr y (1)

d<u>e</u> c<u>ide</u>

d<u>e</u> ci s̲ion   (2)   Rule 13.

en ˙ti ˙tl<u>e</u>₄

po lit i cal

na̱ ˉtion al (1)

na̱ ˉtion

r<u>e</u> cent

bu<u>s</u> i ness   (2)   (Sound as written for spelling. We say "bĭs ness.")

bu<u>s</u> y   (2)

re <u>fer</u>

[min ute₅

  mi nute]

ou⁵ght

[ab sence₃

  ab sent]

[con fer ence₃   (Does not follow Rule 15. The accent shifts to

                con′ and we do not double the r.)

  con fer]

Wed nes day   (Sound as written for spelling. This is Woden's

                day. We say "Wens² day.")

[re al ly

  re al]

cel e bra tion

[fo²lks   (Sound l when spelling.)

  fo²lk]

(This is the point of *minimum* accomplishment for every child in a fifth grade.)

Section U

[me²ant

  mean]

ear li est   Rule 24.

ear ly   (Page 2 in the Notebook.)

wheth er

dis tin guish   (Sound as written for spelling except you say "gw" for gu. We say "dis ting gwish.")

con sid er a tion

col o nies   Rule 24. (Change y to i and add es.)

col o ny

co lo ni al   Rule 24.

as sure   (s says "sh.")

sure

re lief   (Page 3 in the Notebook.)

oc cu py

prob a bly

prob a ble

for eign   (Page 3 in the Notebook. ei says "ī.")

ex pense   Rule 20.

re spon si ble₄

re sponse₅

be gin ning   (Page 5 in the Notebook.)

be gin

ap pli ca tion

ap ply

dif fi cul ty

dif fi cult

scene   (These words use sc to say "s." Since e or i fol-
             lows the c it must say "s." This can be likened
sci ence₃   to ck. c and k alone say "k" and when used to-
             gether they say "k.")
scis sors

de scend

de scent

fi nal ly

fi nal

de vel op

cir cum stance₃   (Page 2 in the Notebook.)

cir cum fer ence₃

cir cle₄

is sue₂   (s says "sh.")

tis sue₂

má te ri al

sug gest

mere

sen ate₅

sen a tor

sen a to ri al

re ceive₂   (Page 3 in the Notebook.)

re spect fúl ly

re spect fúl

re spect

a gree ment

a gree

un for tu nate₅

ma̅ jo̅r i ty

ma jor

e lab o rate₅

cit i zen

cit y

ne̅ ces sa ry

ne̅ ces si ty

di vide

Section V

prin ci pal

prin ci ple₄

tes ti mo ny

dis cus sion   (Page 4 in the Notebook.)

dis cuss

a̅r range ment

a̅r range   (Here two separate consonants come between a which says "a̅" and the final e.)

ref er ence₃   (Rule 15 does not work here. The accent shifted to the first syllable and we do not double the r.)

re fer

ev i dence

ex pe ri ence

ses sion   (Page 4 in the Notebook.)

sec re ta ry

as so ci a tion   (c and i are separate sounds. The syllable says
                  "sĭ.")

ca reer

height   (We write an ā sound but we say "ī.")

weight

Section W

or gan i za tion

or gan ize

e mer gen cy

ap pre ci ate   (Page 4 in the Notebook. Since ci is a syllable
                  alone it says "shĭ" instead of just "sh" as in
                  ancient.)

sin cere ly

sin cere

ath let ic

ath lete

ex treme

prac ti cal

pro ceed

cor di al ly   (Sound as written for spelling. The British say
it this way.)

cor di al

char ac ter

act

sep a rate

Feb ru ar y

li brar y

Section X Y Z

im me di ate

con ven ient   (The i says the consonant y sound as in opinion
shown before.)

re ceipt   (Page 3 in the Notebook. Sound the p for spelling. We do not say it in speech.)

pre limi nar y

dis ap point

> es pe cial ly   (Page 4 in the Notebook.)
>
> spe cial

an nu al

> com mit tee   (Except in a few words (recipē is an exception) we
>   use ee, ea or ey to say "ē" at the end of a word
> em ploy ee   longer than she. Single e's are silent at the end of
>   other words.)
> cof fee

> de ci sion   Rule 13.
>
> de cide

prin ci ple

> judg ment   (dg here does not follow Rule 3. This is an ex-
>   ception. The second spelling in the dictionary re-
> judge   tains the e in dge but it is not commonly used.)

rec om mend

> al lege
>
> al le giance

The sixth-grade work should continue with and complete all of the Buckingham Extension to the *Ayres Spelling Scale.**

This Buckingham Extension adds words which are to be found in sixth-grade books and are needed in writing at that level. The Iowa Spelling Scale by E. J. Ashbaugh published by the University of Iowa at Iowa City is excellent for children who need help in analyzing words beyond those in the Ayres list. There is a separate booklet for each grade from the second to eighth.

The Ayres list is primarily one of base words and may be expanded by adding prefixes and endings. It is interesting to note that we recently had two second-grade classes, each of more than fifty pupils, who completed the Ayres list through the fourth-grade words. More than half made sixth-grade Metropolitan test spelling scores and not one of the 108 scored below beginning fourth grade. Thus children taught by this method do require supplemental word lists beyond the Ayres list for grades beyond the second.

---

*Public School Publishing Co., Bloomington, Ill.

CHAPTER VII

Teaching in the Different Grades

The teachers who use Unified Phonics report that they find it a great advantage to teach all of it to their whole class. The only exception is when they give special time to the group of those having the most difficulty while the others do silent reading or writing. Teaching the whole group not only saves her time but provides the children with the inspiration of learning and working together but independently. This works better by seating the children in separate, orderly rows of individual desks, but in any case all face the teacher.

This seating also enhances the teacher's authority. Most children come to school in the hope of learning,—of being taught. They *want* their teacher to use her authority and teach them. Children desire kind but authoritative discipline from all adults whom they respect.

This all requires much sensitivity and patient determination from the teacher. There come times when she will need to think of the high mission of her profession. She is, in the first grade, usually the first to ask a child to hold himself under sufficient discipline to do something quite new to him,—namely to put his mind to work. That may be his teacher's most valuable lesson for him,—one that she alone can give. The fact that all his classmates are accepting the same discipline and authority at the same time helps him accept it.

212

It is our observation that whole-class teaching, where each child is treated as the equal of all others, is a relief from the constant pressures of the competitive spirit and the efforts of some to dominate others, which often prevail on the playground. There is a very real fascination for young children in learning the basic tools of the written language. When these are well presented children soon acquire enough self-discipline to provide for full attention to the teacher.

With this kind of teaching the child becomes quiet, self-assured, respectful of his teacher and the other children. He constantly competes with himself, trying to better his accomplishment. He accepts any suggestion for improvement gladly for as he reasons, he seeks any new light. Every teacher from the first grade up therefore, should master the basic lessons of how to sit, how to hold a pencil, how to hold and move the paper, how to say the phonograms accurately and how to write the phonograms correctly. Then she should be responsible for seeing that no child is permitted to write without constantly being checked and taught these basic techniques, as detailed in Chapters III and IV.

In classes of up to sixty children we have found all the children eager to be shown ways of improving their work. This attitude is not often found in classes where teachers leave many children in the state that is conveniently labeled *"not ready,"* and where the range of accomplishment is so great that half and more of the children know they are not up to their grade standards. These children are not pleased with themselves, the teacher is not pleased with them, and their parents cannot be proud of their academic accomplishment. A child's mental health is much more assured when he knows he is or has a chance to get abreast of his classmates.

If a child is pleased with his academic accomplishments and still shows personality problems, then the school can look elsewhere for the cause of his problems. However, if he is not doing well in speech, writing and reading the school's first job is to teach the basic techniques to him. A systematic, scientific approach to his learning in school can show him how to attack other problems that beset him. This does not mean the school should not help a child in whatever way it can, but such help should not be a *substitute* for teaching him.

"Handedness" (i.e., being left-handed or right-handed) or "eye-edness" is not important if a child is correctly taught. What the child thinks he has said, seen or heard is important. Left-handed children need have no more difficulty in learning than do others. The directions given on handwriting, except for the position of the paper and for slanting the connected writing, are the same as for the right-handed.

Preschool Training

Nursery-school and kindergarten teachers, and parents at home before children go to school can answer a child's questions on how one says, writes or reads words by studying the previous chapters. Children want to write their own names at age three, four or five. They should be taught how to do so correctly, with a capital for the first letter and lower-case letters for the rest. They should be taught how to sit, hold the paper and the pencil, and how to sound out their own names. Whatever is given them should be intelligible and scrupulously correct.

In kindergarten children can learn to say the individual sounds of the phonogram cards, correlated with the correct writing of the symbols. This gives a basis for correcting their speech as from "stan" to stand, "jist" to just, etc. Children at this age are eager to learn, and if they are correctly taught the basis for a successful school life can be well laid. They come to school so that the teacher will *teach* them— not just to play or to express only that which they already know. Many kindergartens now teach writing and reading.

The First Grade

Learning to say the sounds of the seventy phonograms and learning to write correctly and legibly are two prerequisites to learning to spell and to read.

The teaching of writing, as described in Chapter IV, is combined with the teaching of the sounds of the phonograms right from the start. The teacher will use the blackboard as well as the phonogram cards, and explain the applicable rules.

Some children will write acceptably much sooner than others. As soon as half of the class has acquired enough skill—usually within an aggregate of ten to twelve hours of teaching time—the spelling of simple words should be introduced. Use the Ayres spelling list. The children write about ten new words a day in composition books strictly from the teacher's verbal dictation. Each day after the initial lesson, start with a written test given by dictating the previous day's ten new words in a changed sequence. The test is on a separate paper and the child does not see his errors again. When a child misspells a word on his test paper, the teacher checks this word in the child's notebook where the word is correctly written. He sees only his correct notebook. The checked words are his study lesson.

At every stage, and continuously, the teacher will require each child to *rewrite* each word in which his letters are not well formed or well placed, always asking him to state the rule or rules of writing which he has disregarded. The mental habit to remember and to apply the simple rules about sounding and forming the letters is important. He must learn to think. This is where the teacher must find time to help those who need extra teaching.

The above has to do with the formal spelling lessons. At other times during the day children's interest in how their names are written, words in connection with their play, trips, arithmetic, etc., should be taught. The children do the sounding and write on the board or on paper, with the teacher leading their recall of how the phonograms are made: Mar tha, Phil ip, rab bit, etc. Of course, the children learn that words cannot be written in syllables nor with phonograms underlined, etc. except in writing single words.

When (in about two months from the start of school) the class can read and explain a story of three or four sentences (written on the board without explanations), it is time to give them primers from which to read. It is an error to go too slowly and hold able children back.

The best primer I know is the HERE AND NOW PRIMER by Lucy Sprague Mitchell.* It tells of aspects of New York City which children

* E. P. Dutton, New York, 1936.

find fascinating. It contains no illustrations. The children can draw their own pictures illustrating what they read. All other primers I know of are full of pictures. The children, when reading these, should be led to *read* the story first and *then* look at the pictures to see how well they illustrate the text.

Pictures are of great assistance when talking of something the children have not seen, but certainly no picture is needed for mother, father, cat, dog, house, automobile, etc.

When the first book is presented to a class, it should be read as an adult reads his book. Discuss the author. The children have been writing what *they* say. They have by now read three or four sentences about one subject written on the board by the teacher. They have discussed the meaning of the sentences. Similarly, the author of the book wanted to *talk* to children, so he *wrote* in the book what he wanted to say. He has a name for his book. What does he call it?

Discuss how we talk, not by saying one word at a time, but by saying together the words which go together for the sense of the sentence. How far does the author's first idea go? Where is the first period on the page? That shows where the author's first idea ends. What does the author say in that sentence? Show that the word before a period at the end of a sentence never can be read with the word beginning the next sentence. A comma means that the word before it belongs there for its meaning. The word on the other side belongs there for its meaning. These two words may not be read together if the meaning of the sentence is to be clear. The sense of what is written is partially dependent on understanding the marks of punctuation.

Discuss the child's peripheral vision. Have each child hold his hands far out to the sides, look straight ahead and bring his hands in until he can see the tips of his fingers wiggle. He can see more than a yard across without turning his head. Therefore he can see the whole page at one glance since the page is not more than half a foot across. He can be led to *see* a sentence as a whole and thus read it as a complete thought—not word by word.

Reading first requires actual seeing. Children often insert or substitute their own words, or omit words, in reading. Reading aloud reveals this bad habit. The teacher must ask, "Did you really see what you have just read?" at every such error and have it read correctly. This teaches the important habit of seeing accurately.

Much reading aloud is needed to develop this habit of reading accurately. In reading we are trying to learn from the author and not to substitute our ideas for his.

There is another good reason for more reading aloud; namely, it builds up good enunciation and improves both vocabulary and grammar. It is practice in the skills of reading that we are teaching, as well as learning to get ideas from the printed page. Correct meanings can only be learned from accurate reading. A knowledge of phonics is a prerequisite to accurate reading.

If the children have been properly taught to this point each child in turn should be able to read the ideas presented in the sentences with easy expression. Words that do present a difficulty should be sounded out as they are met. However, in reading *no* sounding out should be done aloud unless the child's silent sounding does not produce the correct word. Many teacher's manuals tell the teacher to present any new words to the class before they are met in the story to be read. They say that the one important thing is to get the meaning of the story. Children should get meaning, of course, but their habits of mind should be considered, too. They should work out the new words as they occur. No one is going to solve all their problems before each assignment when they are a little older. This telling them the new words fosters the mental habit which is seen in many children's inability to stick to an assignment, to concentrate in study periods, or on homework. Children need to be taught ways of meeting problems as they arise and *not* to look for an escape.

If the method given in this book is taught the child obtains in the spelling lesson the basic knowledge of how the written language works and he can figure out almost any word as he comes to it. If he needs some help the teacher helps him only on the individual sound he does not recognize. He should expect to work out each word with the minimum of help.

If by February each year the children have studied the words at least one year beyond the minimum for their grade they find very few words in their reading that they cannot figure out and read.

The teacher's homework is, in part, to see that there are no words in the reading lesson for which she has no explanation as to how they work phonetically.

In a half-hour unrehearsed television program which we gave over an N.B.C. affiliate a *second* grade that had had the Unified Phonics Method from the beginning of grade one read from a *fourth*-grade reader which they had not seen until they read aloud from it on the T.V. program. One boy in reading *buckles,* said "buck, buck, buckles." He was the only one of the fifteen children who found it necessary to sound out a word. He and the others read smoothly and with true expression. They then answered well many questions put to them about what the story told.

I am quoting below from the report of a successful first-grade teacher on how she proceeds in teaching this method to her class of fifty-odd six-year-old children:

On the first day of school I showed the children how they should sit while writing, how to hold the pencil and how to use the "percolator," using the terminology of Mrs. Spalding. That term implies letting what they see or hear percolate (like water through the coffee) into their minds *before* they write or speak. The idea pleases them, and they get the point of thinking first, before acting. At the very beginning the habit of thinking, so necessary to success in learning, is being formed.

After that the single letter cards are the order of the day for about the first month of school. We review each day and add new ones, the number depending on the ability of the class. Provision is made for two half-hour periods each day. During these periods the children say the sounds and write on lined paper. One row at a time also writes on the blackboard. In this way the formation of the letters and the ability of each child to learn are checked.

After a few weeks most of the class is able to follow along as a group, and those who need extra help are singled out. When most of the children have a good idea of the single letter sounds and their correct written forms (that is, they can write them from dictation and not from seeing the cards), I proceed with the words in the Ayres list. The children continue with the other phonograms, for they must know all the sounds *before* the words containing them are presented. The first fifty cards are necessary to write all the first grade words in the Ayres list.

Last year I planned on thirty words a week and found it worked very well. The children sounded and wrote the thirty new words in their notebooks on Monday. We sounded out and then reread the first ten. These the children reviewed for homework. On Tuesday the children were given a twenty word test, ten review words and the ten they had studied. On Tuesday the children studied and sounded the second column of ten. The test on Wednesday included columns 1 and 2. On Friday they were tested on the thirty words. In this way those who were absent for a day or two were able to cover the material they had missed. It also helped the children who needed review. I found when I began to review the first and second grade words at the beginning of February that the children had really grasped them.

This year the children did not start the Pre-primer until November which meant they were then well into the second grade on the *Ayres Spelling List*. At the beginning I divided the class into two groups, 36 in my first group and 18 in my second. This enabled me to give those who needed less teaching a good start and to get them to work independently in their reading workbook. After Christmas when the first group had finished the Primer, I had them review for a week or so until the second group finished. The class started the First Reader together. I took half of the class at a time which, meant only a half hour of teaching daily for each child. The children finished the First Reader before April. Now, in June, they have read the next three books. In reading supplementary material one group in the room never reads aloud a story already read aloud by another group. In this way each child has an opportunity to show he can read independently. All can do this. Some have read many library books during the year and have, because of it, much more expression and fluency. However, *all* can read and *all* comprehend.

At the beginning of February we started to review. Each day the children wrote five first grade words, ten second grade words (all review) and five third grade words (new) in five cent notebooks. These words were sounded by the children individually as they wrote them, then were read without being sounded out, and finally used in a sentence. Tests were given each day. The words spelled incorrectly were checked in their notebook and the per cent of errors written on the top of the page. In this way both children and parents could note progress and review, now and again, those words not mastered. (This would not have been possible if some eighth grade girls had not come to my assistance and corrected the spelling papers each day during their lunch period.)

The children begin after Christmas to compose and write their own sentences. In this way they learn to use a capital where they should and also to use a period or question mark at the end of each sentence. They like to illustrate their sentences in original art, which requires more thought about the meaning of words."

This teacher held a series of after school classes for parents. She taught them this method and they became a very real help, especially for the children who needed it most.

Second Grade

If the class has not been taught the Unified Phonics Method in the first grade, it is necessary to give them the entire first-grade work before going further, but this can be done more rapidly than with a first-grade group of children.

For classes who need only review this can be done in the first few weeks. The teacher will dictate words from the Ayres list and the children will, in concert, write them in composition books. The dictation and writing should be exactly as described by the directions given in Chapter V.

This and constant testing and review should be carried on until the class has learned to write correctly all words in the Ayres list for Grade II to Section M. A complete review should then be given, and for those ready for it the Grade III Ayres list should be started. This goes through Section O. In classes where this method was taught in the first grade many (more than half) have enjoyed working out the words through the fourth grade in the Ayres list. They find few words which are not already in their understanding and speaking vocabulary.

It is important that the teacher remember, at every stage and always, to point out every neglect of any of the rules of pronunciation, of writing, or of spelling which each child's work evidences, and to require him to state the rule and to make the correction himself.

Interesting, well written story books should be read aloud in class by second graders, not just "readers."

The teacher brings background information and explains word meanings so that all children—not just those who will read on their own—get an early experience of reading stories of book length. So much reading in school is in little pieces. Short stories are good if they have some literary value but our aim is to teach the love of fine books.

A teacher reporting in March about her second-year class says that she dictates 20 words each day (the children write them in their note-books). Five words are from the first grade list, five from the second grade list, five from the third grade list and five from the fourth grade list. The first fifteen are review words. The last five are new. The next day they are tested on these.

This class learned cursive writing after Christmas. They said the sounds of the letters in the order in which they appear in the alphabet and learned to connect the manuscript alphabet. (See page 88.) They learned to sound and write the seventy phonograms in cursive writing and then they wrote from dictation the Ayres list from the beginning. Once the cursive writing was introduced they did no more manuscript writing. When the Ayres list was dictated this time the teacher taught them how to add endings to each base word. She dictated the base word and then that word with any common ending: last, lasts, lasted, lasting; old, older, oldest; train, trains, trained, training, trainer, etc.

In dictating words the teacher gives the word but the children give the sentence containing it. The teacher checks their understanding of the words and corrects any slovenly speech or incorrect sentence structure. Grammar is begun even in the first grade.

In February this group began reading from the McCall-Crabbs STANDARD TEST LESSONS IN READING—Book A. They read one lesson a day.

By April every child in this second grade could write at least two or three original sentences on a subject. Many wrote longer stories. In the second grade speech should be perfected. By this time they should know all the sounds, they write and read using precise speech, and this knowledge should be used whenever they speak. Teaching these chil-dren to be aware of the sounds in the words they say as they speak on any subject produces beautiful speech. The slovenly speech now so prevalent can be corrected by the second grade.

Third Grade

The third grade starts with a complete review of the first- and second-grade work. The children write for the first time the seven pages of the Child's Notebook in composition books for reference. Each child also enters in his notebook the words which he misses in the review of the first- and second-grade words from the Ayres list. This is his individual list. All the words of the third- and fourth-grade lists should be dictated by the teacher, and all children write all these words in the notebook. It is essential that the teacher continually repeat the spelling rules, correct the posture and writing habits, and at all times correct the pronunciation and the sounds and spelling of the phonograms.

Those children in the class who may not have had this method in the previous grade will need to start at the beginning and proceed more slowly than the others unless they learn rapidly during the review period at the start of the term.

It is advisable to seat such children and any others who have difficulty near the front where the teacher can supervise and guide them more easily. It has been found entirely practical to let the other children go ahead with reading to themselves and with other such work while the teacher works with the smaller group of children who need to learn spelling commensurate with their grade. All third-graders should learn the words at least to Column R. For most of the class there will be time to go through the rest of the 1000 words in the Ayres list.

The first and second grades need to learn many base words and their endings but the third grade is one where the facts presented on pages 5 and 6 of the child's notebook and explained on pages 112, 113 and 116 should be stressed. The rules on pages 123 to 126 are needed too. Lessons where base words are presented and the children asked to write any word derived from them are excellent for this grade. If mount is given as a base word the children give mounts, mounting, mounted, mounter, mountain, mountains, mountaineer and mountainous. The children may not give a word without being able to put it correctly in a sentence.

It is in the third grade that children like to use the dictionary and find it valuable. They discover the many prefixes and endings for base words as well as the synonyms, and see how the spelling rules for endings apply.

The following is quoted from the report of a third-grade teacher:

For ten years I taught reading by the sight method using the program advocated in the teacher's guide book and followed scrupulously all the so-called "word skills" and "phonetic analysis drills." During this period I used two different readers which, although printed by separate companies, had practically identical systems for presenting vocabulary and word meaning. Likewise during this time I followed two different programs of spelling which stressed oral drill as well as peculiarities in the total word appearance. Five of those years were spent on the mainland and five here in Honolulu. However the entire period although a time of some success for two-thirds of the pupils, was (in the light of my later experiences using the Spalding Method) a time of frustration for one third of my pupils.

Reading, Writing, Spelling, English, and Phonics were each distinct subjects with no unifying bond. But I now find it quite easy to recognize the close connection between the written and spoken sounds in the English language. It seems so ridiculous for a child to read unhesitatingly the word "dog" for "puppy," or "dish" for "plate," and not even realize that he has made a mistake. Oral spelling certainly had its drawbacks too, for at the end of the year only one-fifth of the class were really masters of the four hundred words taught.

Mrs. Spalding's method gives all pupils an independence in attacking new words both in reading and spelling. My present class of sixty-one includes eight brand-new students who were not taught the Spalding method in grades one and two. On the second day of school I gave the Morrison-McCall Graded Spelling test. My median was 4.1, and all my eight new children, plus three of those exposed to the method for two years, were the only ones below 3.1. On October 7, I gave another Morrison-McCall test attaining the median of 5.2, with two of the new pupils still below grade level and also one of my repeaters. From September 1st to November 15th we have covered the entire Ayres list for grades one to three inclusive, and half of grade four.

As for reading comprehension the median on October 3rd was 4.5 and on Nov. 22nd, it reached 5.0. There isn't one non-reader in the class although there are a dozen children whom I give extra help on word meaning. Never do I tell any of the children a word that they can sound by using their phonograms. Exceptions are taught wherever they are met. I still help them on the "ough" card as it is confusing because of the six sounds. As for English Composition, I am simply amazed at what even the slowest can do. Some who learned spelling easily are writing plays. The majority take library books regularly and turn in book reports giving the title, author, characters, and a short appreciation of the book. Many are fast learning the art of using the dictionary to advantage.

Fourth and Higher Grades

Each class reviews and writes again the first seven pages of the Child's Notebook and is tested on the Ayres list from the beginning. Any words from the Ayres list which a child misses in the initial review he puts in his notebook and the teacher finds time to teach these to him as soon as possible. All children put all the words for their own grade and the grade above in their notebook. This shows the teacher where each child and the whole class needs teaching. When this is done, we shall not be sending children with second-grade spelling ability on to higher grades. If they have learned the structure of the language, reading can be taught with ease.

In classes where this method is taught in the first grade each child soon learns to write his own ideas in sentence form. In the second grade by March or April he writes short paragraphs daily. In the third grade he continues this and writes his own book reviews. At no time do the children copy from the board or out of books. Letters to parents and others, reports, etc. are individually composed and written from the start without copying. In the fourth and upper grades we have as many children as there is room for at the blackboard write a paragraph on whatever subject each one chooses. Those not at the board write on paper. This is done every day. Usually each one has selected and studied (but has not written on) his subject as part of his homework. Then the blackboard paragraphs are read aloud and any errors discussed and corrected by the whole class. Those at the desks, having observe the blackboard errors, then revise and correct their own papers before the teacher corrects them. The teacher should help children as to where and how they may find the sources and the information which will make an interesting account. This grade is where the benefits from having read literature of quality should show up in the children's own good taste and good original composition. With this practice it can be hoped that high-school and college students will not dread compositions, nor essay questions in examinations, and that they will be at ease in speaking on subjects of which they have some knowledge. When children ask for the spelling of words they do not know, the teacher asks the child to sound the word and she corrects any inaccurate sounds. The child writes the parts of the word he can and the teacher helps only with those parts he does not know. From third grade on the dictionary should be used when the teacher is not readily available.

Speed reading, which is currently being widely taught, is suitable only, in my opinion, for children who have really learned to read; that is, to read accurately. It is no substitute for the basic teaching of the language subjects.

It should be stated that foreigners studying English will quickly acquire a grasp of our language if it is presented along the lines of this method in the phonetic manner. Without this logical approach English is one of the most difficult languages even for those whose native tongue is a Latin or Germanic language. I have taught a few teachers who are now using it with great success in Japan, the Philippines and in Polynesia.

The teachers using the Unified Phonics Method have found the Morrison-McCall Spelling Scale for Grades 2 to 8 very useful. This scale is published by the World Book Company at Yonkers-on-Hudson, New York, and 2126 Prairie Avenue, Chicago. There are eight parallel tests of 50 words each. Each teacher, beginning in February of the first grade, and in September for the second and subsequent grades, should use one of these tests on the first of each month. This regularly shows how each child is progressing and does not put off until the end of the year learning that some children need special attention.

For reading test lessons we have found McCall-Crabbs STANDARD TEST LESSONS IN READING a great help. There are five booklets for grades 2 through 12. Each booklet contains some 70 paragraphs with about ten questions on each paragraph to be answered. Each test is a three-minute one and the grade scores are given for each test. They are published by Teachers College, Columbia University in New York City.

Unless a teacher has some way of knowing at frequent intervals, other than by subjective judgment, how her children are progressing much time is lost in helping those who need it most.

Many parents have become interested in mastering the techniques of this method and have organized for regular class sessions. These parents are of invaluable assistance to teachers.

When I have taught individual children who have difficulty in the language subjects, I have required that the parents of children of elementary-school age especially work with the child and me through the lessons so that they can help their children at home. This can make for a strong bond between children and parents. When a parent does not know how to help, he is placed in the unhappy role of a taskmaster. Teachers should feel responsible to parents for giving them any information they have which parents can use at home to help their children learn.

So many parents have told me that primary teachers say to them, "Don't teach your child at home. You will only confuse him. Let the school teach him to read." Then when the school has not taught him to read, teachers say, "Help him at home," or "Get a tutor for him." They often give the parents no idea as to *how* to help and no word as to just what the tutor should do. There is much untapped assistance for the teacher in the parents of the children who need more help if these parents are taught how.

How should each child study the words he misses?

1) Read the word carefully, sounding each sound of a one-syllable word and each syllable of a polysyllabic word.

2) Cover the word and write it in syllables, sounding the individual phonograms or syllables.

3) Check to see that the word is correct. This self-testing habit is very important.

4) Do this with each word to be learned.

5) Ask a reliable person at home or in school to test him on the new words exactly as tests are given in class.

6) The tester should check the paper as the teacher does.

7) The child immediately restudies by writing the words missed.

8) Repeat these tests until the child no longer makes errors in writing these words.

9) Bring to class the next day the study sheets, the home test, and further study sheets if any.

Here is something definite which teachers can teach parents. They can invite parents to the children's classrooms and have them participate in the lessons. They learn how to hold the paper and the pencil, how to sit, how to form the letters, saying the sound before the writing of each phonogram. The teachers explain how spelling is taught and just how the parents can help their children in reading, in spelling or in speech. In the end this cooperation relieves the teacher of much special attention to pupils who need the most help.

The sixth-grade children should have had enough teaching in basic grammar to be able to analyze and identify the grammatical parts of almost any sentence. This may require a textbook grammar or not, as the teacher prefers. The understanding of grammar helps their ability to express their ideas in writing, and to see the difference between a good author and one less competent.

High-school students who have not been taught by this method can benefit greatly from it as the following quotation from a teacher's recent report indicates:

After two months' work last fall with my five senior English classes, I realized that the students were not able to go ahead with a regular 12th grade curriculum without special assistance from somewhere. They misspelled simple words. Most of them approached English and reading—as though it were impossible of comprehension by any normal being.

The teaching of Old and Middle English literature to people who could not read present-day English was highly improbable and I found the students blithely flunking exams with grades of 10 and 20 rather than attempting to do the homework connected with literature.

Some of them could quote grammar rules, name parts of speech and even diagram sentences with easy fluency but they could not write. I found I could not teach composition because they did not have the tools for self-expression.

Vocabulary was just as hopeless. They reacted with resentment when they found that there were shades of meaning for the correct usage of a word.

The first spelling tests I gave showed the same incomprehension. After the first two letters, a word, to most of them, was simply a wild jumble of letters which carried no meaning either to their eyes or their ears.

The result was that I stopped all regular work in English and started the students out on a six-weeks' course of Mrs. Spalding's method. We made notebooks, using the first seven pages as a graphic presentation of the rules of spelling. Then we started on lists of spelling words which commenced with grade 1.

Although they started the new regime somewhat rebelliously, the students soon recognized that the sounding of the letters was not only teaching them spelling, but correct speech sounds without the embarrassment of working in front of a group. As they began to comprehend the letters by sound, the English language began to fall into order in their minds and they began to find that they had a whole new grasp of their own language. This was apparent to me in the growing unity and cooperation in the classes. For the first time I was not pulling against them.

Soon students began coming to my desk and expressing appreciation of the work I was giving them, telling me that they had never been taught like that before. One boy told me, "If I could spell, I could learn to read!"

The results of the first spelling test showed that the average grade level of these senior high school students was between sixth- and seventh-grade. If I had given the first test before we started on Mrs. Spalding's regime, the average would have been probably at fifth grade. On the second test, given a month later, the average rose about half a grade level. But the mistakes consisted of only one letter in a three-, four-, or five-syllable word. The average of the class in spelling has risen steadily until time for their college entrance examinations.

About one-third of the whole senior class has taken the college entrance examinations (the highest number yet to do so in the history of the school).

The good students have become much more secure; the poor students are by now passing in their 12th grade work. None of this would have been possible if I had not been able to give the students a grounding in the English language. During the first two months I was failing with them, as other teachers before me had failed. And I would still be failing if I had not had this concise, logical and most readily teachable method to present to my classes. Giving my students this work has solved not only their most obvious problems in speech and the use of English but also the more subtle problems of courtesy and class behavior. I simply do not have the disciplinary problems that bedevil so many of my colleagues.

CHAPTER VIII

Specific Disabilities

THERE IS ONE more phase of teaching the English language which requires special mention.

Teachers in all grades encounter many children with definite reading or spelling handicaps. Dr. Orton evolved his method—which is essentially the basis on which I have developed my method of teaching *all* children—to overcome these handicaps in children having severe disabilities. Some insight into his discoveries and teaching will be helpful to both parents and teachers of such children.

Following World War I Dr. Orton discovered that soldiers who had lost the ability to speak, read or write because of head wounds could regain these abilities by certain training. In brief, he learned that on both sides of the human brain there is a center where the picture of words seen on the printed page is recorded and where meaning is given to them. On one side the image is in reverse from that recorded on the other side. Therefore one side should become the dominant one, the one habitually used. Which side is the dominant one is a matter of inheritance much as (although entirely independent of) inherited left-handedness or right-handedness. If the other, or less dominant, side is sometimes used the child records the letter or letters in reverse. At such times the young child mistakes b for d, was for saw, on for no, etc. Al-

230

though the older child may learn to correct this for short words he becomes utterly confused by longer ones. His reading (and spelling) is thus, in many instances, pure guesswork. These children have simply inherited a tendency to use not one side, but either side of the brain for identifying meaning with the printed words seen. The same sort of confusion occurs with children who cannot decide whether to jump from the right foot or the left. They are not well coordinated in certain physical efforts. Motor patterns are stored in other areas of the brain, but in the same way that the symbols of written language are recorded. This is why it is necessary to teach handwriting—the motor patterns— so thoroughly.

This tendency to use sometimes one, sometimes the other side of the brain, and sometimes both at once in reading can only be overcome by training these children to use habitually one side only. This is done by reinforcing their uncertain visual recall with the use of their aural recall and their kinesthetic controls. The latter are usually not uncertain when the visual recall is. For that reason the child is taught to use the muscles of his mouth to say the word, and those of his hand to write it, and he hears it at practically the same time that he sees his own writing of it. That is why children should say a syllable just before they write it. Suffice it to say that, regardless of theory, this process actually works and works infallibly for all children.

Some, of course, need more of this training than others. Note that the teacher quoted in the previous chapter gave eighteen children in her group more of this basic training, while the thirty-six others went ahead more rapidly until the eighteen caught up. It takes much longer for these children to acquire a dominant side of the brain if they start this training in later years.

Fully one-fourth of any group tends to have, under today's teaching methods, this sort of reading disability and barely ten per cent are likely to be entirely free from it. It has nothing to do with a child's intelligence. I have tested literally hundreds of slow readers and found this tendency to be confused and similar signs of this particular trouble in nearly every one. Thus it is not remedial teaching for a few, but a suitable method for all, and the elimination of all remedial reading cases, which we should aim for, especially since this method of teaching is no handicap to any, and is fundamentally sound for every child.

I have just tested a bright boy entering third grade who had not been taught by this method. His tests showed the typical errors of a child with this specific confusion in language. In reading he scored 1.4 instead of 3.0. Some of his errors were that he read dig, big; dug, bus; cart, card; of, from; who, will; how, low; tan, tell; tap, teeth; done, doing; left, light; form, from; balk, black; pig, big; sung, sun; and send, san.

In spelling he scored 1.9. He wrote soft, sf; spent, sbt; deep, be; stay, stat; upon, ap; street, steen; and his name Clarke, Clke and then Clkic. He made most of the horizontal lines backwards. These errors are clear evidence of the source of his trouble. His visual recall of what he reads is often in reverse; and his inability to express in letters the sounds of words in his spelling is apparent.

It is interesting to note that Dr. Orton and most other students of this problem have concluded that this confusion in the visual recall of words read is inherited through the maternal side, as is color-blindness. This is said to account for the fact that about four times as many boys as girls have serious trouble in reading. I believe it is a fallacy that this reading difference is caused by a slower maturing of boys' minds. As I have said, the weight of evidence indicates that every school child is physically and mentally mature enough to read at about the age of six.

We have not said much about the fact that good speech, at least as regards accurate, clear pronunciation, is essential to the best results from this method of teaching, and is its most valuable by-product. Otto Jespersen said, as quoted earlier, that in English the consonants are clearly and concisely pronounced. Yet today in America, as another scholar points out, how many teachers have fallen into the current lazy habit of pronouncing consonants in a slovenly and indecisive manner. Many people reduce to a minimum the movements of the organs of speech, and their language becomes a confused noise of words, so indistinguishable as to be very difficult to understand.

I can compare the ease with which a large audience understood the speaking (without loudspeakers) of the English concert comedienne, Anna Russell, and the great difficulty in understanding a very eminent American doctor, speaking with the latest amplifying devices in an acoustically perfect auditorium to a much smaller audience.

If our consonants are being slighted in American speech how much more are we neglecting the accurate sounds of the vowels. The one sound "uh" is frequently substituted for many of the true vowel sounds. Our American spoken language has been rapidly deteriorating, and this has probably come about chiefly through the fact that this generation has been given no clear understanding of the phonetic basis of English. The relation between the spelling and the pronouncing of every word has not been taught or even explained. That relationship, however, is the key to this method of teaching, and accurate speaking is a definite, important part of this teaching. It should be said further that the habit of using clear, easily understood speech is a real aid to clear thinking. Also, while it may not exactly win friends, it certainly helps in influencing other people. The standards of accurate pronunciation which a teacher requires of her pupils are really a very important part of their education. It may not be too late to stem the present trend in America toward the serious deterioration of our spoken language.

On this point teachers and educators need to know that the dictionary upholds no standard of pronunciation. Instead its only aim is to reflect the average pronunciation of educated people, including some parts of their present slovenly and deteriorating speech in the United States. We ought therefore to speak more precisely than the dictionary indicates—that is, to follow more precisely the correct vowel sounds and avoid the slurring of consonant sounds.

Children who have inherited the tendency to severe language disabilities will overcome this in the first grade if properly taught, but if this method is not available for them until much later on they will still overcome it with good classroom teaching and a little home cooperation. They should not need any remedial teaching by a special teacher.

CHAPTER IX

Ultimate Objectives

IT HAS BEEN my objective to write a book which is constructive, to give parents, teachers and educators, and our children something directly useful. I have tried to avoid the more exhilarating process of deflating the various false gods of language teaching to whom so many educators make obeisance. Other books have ably exposed the serious failure of current reading methods, and it has been my purpose to present a solution to the problem. It is my hope that this resulting book is sufficiently complete and clear to enable both teachers and parents to follow and teach from it accurately without any added instruction.

In the very interesting scheme of things, whereby mankind individually spends but a few days, relatively speaking, on this fairly permanent globe, it naturally befalls us to pass on to children what we have learned in life. Otherwise mankind recedes instead of advancing towards its ever expanding destiny.

But teaching is not only the most important duty of each generation; it is also the most delicate of all arts. A gifted teacher always needs to be extremely sensitive to her pupils' emotional and mental processes. What holds their attention, what best reaches their understanding, what helps them retain, what inspires them to make use of and apply regularly all that they learn?

It has been of absorbing interest to learn some of the answers to these questions by careful trial and error in the field of teaching language. I have approached the problems on the perhaps unfair assumption that all big and little prevailing ideas on how to teach every part of language ought to prove out under test, and that minor, if not major, improvements might be attained by careful testing in practice.

That is why this book may seem to parents and to some trained teachers to be unnecessarily full of detailed teaching techniques. All of them are, however, good working techniques and worth recording.

As I have said repeatedly, our immediate aim is the teaching of accurate speaking, good handwriting, correct spelling and easy, rapid and fully understood reading, but it cannot be said that this is our final objective. These are only the tools to which every child is entitled and which are absolutely essential to the mental and spiritual development of his maximum inherent abilities. Many other things are needed to bring forth the best in a man, but without these basic tools at his command he cannot begin to realize his natural capabilities. Many fine minds are denied their full growth and contributions to mankind simply because they lack mastery of these basic means of communication from others (as in reading), and with others (as in speaking and writing).

Let me illustrate how an early mastery of the language arts by a class provided enough free time so that I was able to teach history and related subjects in the manner which I think is ideal. My sixth-grade group of 32 in the Bronxville Public School near New York City read aloud together six excellent story books on the Middle Ages.

I purchased seventeen copies of each and had two children sit together as we read them. Each of these books was very well written.

We thus built a *common* background on the Middle Ages. We said such words as *tournament, battlements, moat, illuminated manuscript, scriptorium, falcon;* and for each concept I had scoured the old bookshops of New York for the best illustrations available. Old illustrated musical periodicals yielded some beautiful pictures of monastic life in color. Art books had reproductions in color of Brother Stephen's illuminations for the very Hour Book told of in GABRIEL AND THE HOUR BOOK by Evaleen Stein (L. C. Page, Boston). Each picture was of artistic merit.

I took a course for teachers at the Metropolitan Museum of Art on background material that the Museum offered, to make such studies as the medieval period come alive for children. The staff at the Museum also provided invaluable bibliography and source material. At Columbia University I took many courses in Industrial Arts. I learned how the monks made ink and paints, how to bind a medieval book, how to weave a small Oriental rug, how to weave a small Gobelin tapestry, how to work in metal and with leather, how to make the natural dyes as they were made in the Middle Ages, how to make stained glass, etc. These crafts were to be used for true education work. The intellectual content was unbelievably rich.

These studies together with my straight history courses made my sixth-grade students able to enjoy our work on the Middle Ages. They formed guilds, made banners, wrote their laws, became apprentices, journeymen and master craftsmen in weaving, dyeing, metalwork, leatherwork, etc. They saw how these guilds were the forerunners of today's labor unions. Each child made a cartoon, using appropriate subject matter. Then with the same number of warp threads to the inch and the same kind and weight of wool as those in the Metropolitan Museum, each student wove a tapestry about five by eight inches. When we visited the Museum they all had some idea of the work involved in making those beautiful tapestries. Each child wrote, illuminated and bound a book. When we went to the Pierpont Morgan Library and saw probably the finest collection of illuminated books in the world, they looked at them with genuine appreciation.

The children embroidered, using long, narrow cloth and wool of the same colors as were used in the Bayeux tapestry. Our tapestry told the story of GABRIEL AND THE HOUR BOOK instead of the Norman Conquest.

At the end of the year the children wrote and produced a play using properties we had been making. The pupils' language was colored by the fine writings we had read together.

Some children read as many as fifty books on the Middle Ages. I had seen to it that they had the kind of knowledge which made exciting and interesting reading of such books as THE STORY OF KING ARTHUR AND HIS KNIGHTS by Howard Pyle (Scribners, New York).

I have written briefly on what my sixth-grade class in history did to show how one of the real interests in teaching is to give children a share in our great cultural heritage. This group learned dozens of our finest poems—poems they will be proud to know when they are many years older. They wrote copiously on their experiences and on the books they read independently. They learned and their interests expanded and they took on new depths of understanding, not only of history but of the present-day world. They learned something about the start of this scientific era and developed this further in their science classes.

What has all this to do with phonics? The answer is simply this: Without a working knowledge of how to speak, write and read any child is severely handicapped in learning of and understanding his cultural heritage.

Such studies can be started as early as the third grade. For example, third-graders can carry out a rich study of the American Indians with real intellectual content. After reading aloud together books that give in story form the lives of the various tribes and studying geography which partly explains why one tribe lived quite differently from another, children can then read individually as many as a hundred books on Indians. One of my third-graders did just that by February of one year. He was quite an authority for an eight-year-old. An excellent series for reading aloud together are the books on Indian life by Sonia Bleeker (William Morrow & Co., New York). THE INDIAN'S SECRET WORLD by Robert Hofsinde (William Morrow & Co., 1955) is an excellent source book.

All children can enjoy enriched education if speech, writing, spelling and reading are taught in the first two years by the method recommended in this book. Those who cannot speak well, read intelligently and write well hold back the imparting of knowledge and true education to the whole class. When we water down education to the level of those who present learning difficulties, we neglect the education of those who learn with ease. Thus the true objective for a teacher is to avail herself of the means of raising the standards of all children in a group so that all may enjoy a good education.

This sort of enriched teaching in the elementary school prepares children to study intelligently straight history, economics, foreign languages and similar courses in high school.

These supplementary parts of teaching are obviously open to parents, just as the techniques in this book of teaching the language arts can be taught at home. Even when children may be taught in the classroom it is a great help to have parents understand and cooperate at home.

An educator has recently written, "It is hoped that some day education will throw away meaningless generalizations and concentrate critically upon the learning that takes place." That has been my endeavor. I also agree with him that teaching should provide each child with the tools and interests which enable him to learn and grow intellectually. A democracy especially requires a type of universal education which will develop in each individual his maximum ability for understanding and sound thinking.

As I write this closing word, I have just come home from teaching this method to two classes, a total of 445 teachers and principals, one class in Ohio and one in California. It required forty hours in class to prepare them to teach it to children successfully. I estimate that a serious student of this book will need the same time to achieve a similar ability to teach it.

It is thus our hope that the book may, in effect, enable anyone or any groups of teachers and parents to learn and use this method. It follows then that our major objective in this undertaking may be accomplished.

This objective is to help prevent the unhappiness and the appalling loss caused by so large a proportion of our people living and thinking, working and producing, at levels so far below their inborn mental abilities, because of their relative inability to read and write. As a corollary to this objective we also hope for an important up-grading in the average standards of scholarship and educational objectives in all our schools and colleges. We believe we have presented in this book one indispensable, basic step toward attaining these two great goals.

APPENDIX
A Guide for Teachers

APPENDIX

A Teacher's Guide for Teaching from *The Writing Road to Reading*

This guide is basic for teaching any class of children beginning, or continuing, to learn the Unified Phonics method, either in first grade or in higher grades. It has proved best to move forward rapidly with the drill in the phonogram sounds and handwriting—two of the basic tools—not expecting these to be learned *fully* by every child before he starts the writing of words and the reading of them. Children then realize the need of these tools and continue to work hard to acquire them, and to use them. Extra practice time for some children is essential. Teachers will note that the Unified Phonics method progresses at a much faster pace than most others do.

I. *Introduction*

The teacher should *review* and *study* pages 37 to 42 with special attention to the first paragraph on page 40.

II. *Single-Letter Phonograms*

Present the standards and techniques for correct writing just as described from the bottom of page 68 to page 73. Call attention to each of these details frequently each day until good writing habits are acquired.

Begin actual writing as described on page 74 and proceed with the class writing the phonograms including the numerals and capitals as needed, all as described on pages 75 to 87. Have the whole class say the sounds of each phonogram in review daily until all know them.

Present four to nine new phonograms each day according to class ability. Each day review all techniques, phonograms and words presented on the previous day.

All single-letter phonograms can be presented in three to five days. Continue daily practice, using a different sequence of phonograms. Use the writing, spelling, language, and reading periods for this work at the beginning, until the phonograms are mastered. It is well to use three or four separate thirty-minute periods a day for this practice.

III. *Dictation*

As soon as all the children have learned a few phonograms, begin dictating them. Children write the phonogram from hearing the sounds, and do not see the card. This can be started on the fourth or fifth day. Immediately after they write the phonogram write it on the board, so that children who may have made errors can correct them at once.

Correct at all times each child's failure to follow all the writing rules described on pages 68–87 until good basic writing habits and the sounds of these phonograms are well established. One test is the children's ability to write the phonograms from dictation.

Then proceed to teach the rest of the first fifty-four phonograms in the same manner, pages 51 to 60.

IV. *Spelling Words*

The children are now ready to analyze and to write in notebooks words from dictation—pages 130, 131, etc.

Study and teach, when met, the phonogram underlining and numbering given on pages 127 to 131. Also learn and, when and as met with in words, teach thoroughly the twenty-eight spelling rules on pages 123 to 126. These rules soon come to be memorized by the children but are first shown to them by the teacher, as they come up in spelling words, as facts which they should know about our language.

V. *The Child's Notebook—Page One*

Page 99 (Page 1 of the third-grade Child's Notebook) should be put on two charts (by the teacher in a first or second grade)—one chart for the twenty-six letters and one for the silent final *e*'s.

Follow carefully the notes to teachers, pages 98 to 101.

Use of the blackboard by groups of children is a very effective means of teaching. Those not at the board write on paper at their seats.

Teach the charts and teach the words, as directed (pages 127–131) from the Ayres list in sequence—averaging up to thirty new words per week. Note that *each* child gives an original sentence to show the meaning of each new word.

This requires teaching more phonograms *before* they arise in new words. A daily review of all the sounds from the phonogram cards previously taught is advisable.

VI. *Writing Sentences*

Children begin writing their own sentences when they have completed the first-grade spelling words of the Ayres list (page 142) and are well into the second-grade words. They must have sufficient background in spelling so that they can be successful in writing their own sentences. The daily practice in giving good oral sentences has paved the way for understanding what a good sentence is.

VII. *Reading Sentences* (Using Spelling Words)

When they have written sentences the children read them aloud from their papers and read each other's as written on the blackboard. From the very beginning, meaning is stressed in every spelling lesson and in the writing and reading of sentences.

Daily practice on the phonogram sounds continues with the spelling words until a thorough mastery of the phonograms has been achieved by all. Not all will need the same amount of practice, and no child should be held for practice after he has mastered the phonograms.

VIII. *The Child's Notebook Continued*

When page 136 is reached it is time to put the top sentence of page 2 of the "Child's Notebook" (pages 102–105) on a chart and to teach the five spellings of the sound of *er*. Enter each new word with this sound in the appropriate column on this chart.

If it has not been needed earlier, page 6 of the Child's Notebook (see pages 116–117) will be taught to explain the word *coming* in the Ayres list, page 157. Put such words on a chart as they are needed.

At this time page 5 of the Child's Notebook also should be taught and put on a chart. (See pages 112–115.)

IX. *Reading from Books*

In first grade the children begin to read aloud from books of literary merit (not only basal readers) when they are well into the second-grade words of the Ayres list. Each child holds a copy and follows the reader. The subject matter should have educational value, such as history, science, etc. See page 219. The time for beginning to read books will vary. Most classes will be ready for books in early November. Pages 215–217.

Correct pronunciation is always required.

Children begin individual silent reading of suitable, selected books of real literary merit from the school library by April in the first grade, and this reading is more and more required in each higher grade.

The teacher will understand the difficulties which a large percentage of her pupils have to overcome by studying Chapter VIII, "Specific Language Disabilities." This enables her to explain matters to parents of children who have difficulty, and thus to enlist their help at home. This help to children who need special attention is a useful part of the Unified Phonics Method. Parents study it and, under the teacher's guidance, can be a great help to their children.

X. *Continued Work in First Grade*

Proceed with the words of the Ayres list, reviewing all the previous phonogram sounds and frequently adding more phonograms and the spelling rules as they apply. When the word *died* is met on page 170 this calls for page 3 of the Child's Notebook, with its chart. (See pages 104–107.)

All seventy phonograms will be well learned during the first grade. This requires the teaching of page seven of the Child's Notebook, pages 118–122. It may be desirable to teach page 4 of the Child's Notebook (pages 108–111) if the class has advanced far enough. The first grade should complete the Ayres-list words down to Section M, page 165, by February. Start children writing several original sentences on some subject before midyear—page 219. Then review all words. Many first grades add new words down to Section P on page 182.

Further suggestions about teaching the first grade will be found on pages 214–219. In the first and second grades teach the ideas, but omit many of the mature example words that are given on pages two to six of the Child's Notebook.

XI. *The Second Grade and Beyond*

The second grade begins with a full review of the first-grade work and then proceeds in the same manner with thirty new words of the Ayres list each week. After Christmas holidays cursive writing is taught just as outlined on pages 88–93. The second grade should complete all words in the Ayres list down to Section P, page 182, by February. They then review all words and many classes can add new words. Much more reading aloud in class of good books and more writing of original compositions is done in each higher elementary grade.

The third grade should review all words and complete down to Section R, page 193, by February. Each third-grade child should write his own Child's Notebook, seven pages, fully correct for use as his own reference book when needed.

The fourth-grade classes should review all words and complete the Ayres list by February.

Teachers should all read and make use of the teaching suggestions given in Chapter VII, "Teaching in the Different Grades," pages 221–227.

More reading aloud in class is needed in the upper grades.

Original written compositions are also expanded into written stories and articles more and more in each higher grade.

In the fifth and higher grades start the school year with a rapid review of the phonograms, the writing techniques, the spelling rules and the vocabulary, which at the sixth grade will include the words of the Buckingham Extension to the Ayres list—page 211.

Some of the ideas for collateral education as discussed in Chapter IX, pages 233–238, should be introduced in the upper elementary grades.